THE BELIEFNET GUIDE TO

Gnosticism

and Other

Vanished

Christianities

Also available

THE BELIEFNET GUIDE TO KABBALAH

THE BELIEFNET GUIDE TO EVANGELICAL CHRISTIANITY

THE BELIEFNET GUIDE TO ISLAM

THE BELIEFNET GUIDE TO

GNOSTICISM AND OTHER VANISHED CHRISTIANITIES

Richard Valantasis

Preface by
Marcus Borg

Three Leaves Press

Doubleday / New York

THREE
LEAVES
PRESS

PUBLISHED BY DOUBLEDAY
a division of Random House, Inc.

THREE LEAVES PRESS and its colophon are trademarks of
Random House, Inc., and DOUBLEDAY and its colophon are
registered trademarks of Random House, Inc.

Library of Congress Cataloging-in-Publication Data

Valantasis, Richard, 1946–
   The Beliefnet guide to Gnosticism and other vanished
Christianities / by Richard Valantasis ; preface by Marcus
Borg.—1st Three Leaves Press ed.
      p.   cm.—(The Beliefnet guides)
   1. Gnosticism. 2. Heresies, Christian—History—Early
church, ca. 30-600. 3. Church history—Primitive and early
church, ca. 30-600. I. Title. II. Series.

BT1390.V35 2006
299'.932—dc22   2005050577

ISBN 0-385-51455-7
PRINTED IN THE UNITED STATES OF AMERICA

First Three Leaves Press Edition

10 9 8 7 6 5 4 3 2 1

CONTENTS

6. Feeling the Burn: Ascetic Christianity and the Quest for Bodily Purity

7. Holy Rollers and Sacred Terrorists

8. Challenges to Christianity from the Roman World

This book on "vanished Christianities" puts us in touch with forms of early Christianity that did not survive. It thus describes directions Christianity could have taken but didn't.

Scholars and some Christians have become increasingly aware of early Christian diversity over the past few decades. Until about a half century ago, we knew about these groups primarily from their Christian opponents. But in 1945, an early Christian library from the fourth century was discovered in southern Egypt. It contained fifty-one Christian documents from the first few centuries of Christianity, most of them hitherto unknown. They were published in English translation in 1977 as *The Nag Hammadi Library.*

At about the same time, Elaine Pagels's book *The Gnostic Gospels* became a bestseller. More recently, her book *Beyond Belief* (another bestseller) contrasts the *Gospel of Thomas* with the Gospel of John as two very different forms of early Christianity. Along with Bart Ehrman's *Lost Christianities,* it has once again brought early Christian diversity to public attention.

This book by Richard Valantasis not only stands in the same

genre, but also makes a major contribution to our awareness of the varieties of early Christianity. Such awareness is both interesting and important, especially for Christians, and for both historical and contemporary reasons.

To begin with why it's interesting, here you will meet "vanished" voices from the first three centuries of Christianity. In this book, to mention only a few of the Christian groups that Valantasis describes, we meet:

- Valentinian Christians (second century): an elite intellectual group who devised a sophisticated allegorical and spiritual interpretation of scripture.
- Marcionite Christians (second century): a group who rejected Jewish scripture (what Christians now call the Old Testament) and the God of Judaism, and produced a "New Testament" consisting only of a highly edited version of Luke's gospel and a collection of Paul's letters.
- Montanist Christians (second and third centuries): a charismatic Spirit-filled "radical feminist" group (to use Valantasis' language) that ordained women as deacons, priests, and bishops.
- Donatist Christians (early fourth century): a rigorous group that rejected any Christians who had collaborated with Rome during the great persecution of the early 300s, and whose "terrorist wing," the Circumcellions, physically attacked collaborationist Christians even as they also sought martyrdom.

You will also encounter early Christian documents from this period that did not make it into the New Testament: the *Gospel of Mary, Gospel of Thomas, Gospel of the Savior, Secret Gospel of Mark,* and so forth.

These vanished forms of Christianity invite speculation about "counterfactual" history. Such history imagines what the world would be like if the historical process had developed differently. For example, what would our world be like if Hitler had vanquished the Russians by beginning his Russian campaign a month earlier in 1941 so that he could have conquered Leningrad and Moscow before the Russian winter set in? Or, to use Philip Roth's most recent novel *The Plot Against America* as an example: What would have happened if an isolationist and Nazi sympathizer had won the presidential election against Franklin Roosevelt in 1940?

Valantasis engages in such "counterfactual" speculation in his engaging opening chapter, in which he imagines what Christian congregational life today might be like if one or another of these groups had continued as the road most taken.

An awareness of early Christianities is not only interesting but important and helpful. For Christians in particular, it matters for more than one reason.

Many of the questions that Christians struggled with in the first three centuries are still with us:

- Is the Bible to be interpreted only literally, or may it be interpreted metaphorically and spiritually?
- How should Christians live in a dominant culture whose values are radically different from the

Christian vision? Is Christianity primarily about an inner spiritual freedom that can accommodate itself to any dominant culture, or does it also lead to resistance to dominant culture? In early Christianity, the dominant culture was the Roman Empire. In our time, it is modern Western culture coupled (for Americans) with imperial power. How much can Christians compromise with culture, with "the world," and still be Christian?

· How much should the sacred scripture of Judaism—what Christians call the Old Testament—matter to Christians? Probably at least a slight majority of Christians today are "Marcionite" without being aware of it. There is a widespread Christian stereotype that contrasts the God of the Old Testament as a God of law and judgment with the God of the New Testament as a God of mercy and love. This contrast is implicit Marcionitism, even as it is also wrong. To "demote" the God of the Old Testament impoverishes our understanding of the Bible and Christianity.

There is yet another reason that awareness of early Christian diversity matters. Namely, we are living in a time of major change (and thus conflict) within North American Christianity. A way of being Christian (which I call "an earlier Christianity") has ceased to be persuasive to millions of people in our time, including many who are Christians as well as many who have left the church or never been part of it.

Another way of being Christian (which I call "an emerging

Christianity") is being embraced by many within the church. Opponents of this change frequently defend their form of Christianity as being "traditional" Christianity, that is, as *the* right way of being Christian, *the* correct form of Christianity.

But this book makes us aware that there has never been *one* single form of Christianity. As Valantasis emphasizes, we mistakenly tend to think of Christian diversity as a relatively late development. Our commonly told story portrays the church and Christianity as a unified institution until the eleventh century, the period of "the one true church." Then in 1054 the great division between western (Roman Catholic) and eastern (Orthodox) Christianity occurred. Some centuries later, in the Protestant Reformation of the sixteenth century, western Christianity divided again, eventually into hundreds of denominations, many of them seeking to return to the "pure" form of Christianity of the New Testament and the earliest centuries.

But there were many forms of Christianity from its earliest days. There have been many ways of being Christian from the beginning. No one way can claim to be the only way. So also in our time: no particular form of Christianity can claim to be the only true form, the only right way.

This awareness raises another question: Are there some ways of being Christian that aren't really Christian? To put that differently, is every group that claims the name "Christian" authentically Christian?

I don't have a precise answer. But two things seem clear to me. On the one hand, there are differences that do not disqualify one from being Christian. I use as an example the famous conflict between two Christian leaders of the early fourth century, Arius and Athanasius. They were the primary antagonists at the Council of Nicaea in 325 c.e., the council (as this book notes) that created most of the Nicene Creed that is used in churches to this day.

At the center of the controversy was the ultimate status of Jesus. For both Athanasius and Arius, Jesus was utterly central. But was Jesus one with God, of the same substance as God, co-eternal with God, part of the Trinity (Athanasius)? Or was Jesus of utmost importance but nevertheless a little bit less than God, created and not co-eternal (Arius)?

Athanasius and his position won. But does this mean that Arius wasn't really or authentically Christian? My own answer: of course Arius was a Christian. The difference between him and Athanasius wasn't great enough to disqualify him as a Christian. In general, doctrinal differences like this do not seem to me to be the determining factor in whether a person or position is Christian.

On the other hand, it seems equally clear to me that there are groups and theologies that claim to be Christian that are not. To use two obvious examples, the Branch Davidians convened by David Koresh and white supremacist "Christian" groups are far beyond anything recognizably Christian. About such groups, it is not difficult to say, "Not Christian."

Of course, those are the easy cases. But they do suggest that there are boundaries to what can be called Christian, even as those boundaries should not be narrowly drawn.

Discernment about the boundaries of authentic forms of Christianity is less clear when we think about some of the forms of early Christian diversity that Valantasis reports. For example, several of these groups disparaged the material world as being the creation of an inferior god, a god who was evil, and not the true God. So, do we say, "These people denied that the world was created by God, and therefore they weren't Christian"? Or do we say, "These were Christians who denied that the material world was the good creation of God"?

Such discernment is difficult. But according to a saying of Jesus reported in Matthew's gospel, the primary test of discernment is "By their fruits, you shall know them." The fruits are often very mixed in the lives of most Christians. Of the Christians whom Valantasis describes, we know very little about the virtues their lives embodied. Most of them viewed the world as evil. But were their lives filled with compassion, in spite of their frequent disparagement of the world as evil? Or were their lives filled with judgmentalism, grounded in spiritual elitism or unredeemed anger or both? Would we see among them, if we knew more about them, the lives of saints?

Thus also in our time, the test of "authentic" Christianity is "By their fruits, you shall know them." The Spirit of God can and does work through a variety of ways.

So, I welcome you to this book. Read it to satisfy your curiosity about these vanished forms of Christianity, including some very strange ones. And use it to reflect about what it means to be religious today by struggling with the questions that faced them.

In the first centuries after the crucifixion of Jesus, a rich variety of beliefs and practices developed throughout the ancient world, many of them Christian in name but startlingly different from what we think of as Christianity today. Members of long-forgotten Christian movements created dauntingly complex philosophical systems—some of which describe the world as the creation of a lesser God and Jesus as a mortal man. There were pious monks who sat on pillars in the desert; others crawled about on their hands and knees eating grass to save the world; still others regarded flatulence as an audible sign of divine grace. There were ascetics and libertines; biblical fundamentalists and revisionists—some extremists even perpetrated acts of suicidal terrorism.

Until recently these alternative forms of Christianity were hardly discussed outside of academia. Their ideas and beliefs have become much better known in recent years, not only through serious-minded popularizations by highly regarded scholars like Elaine Pagels and Bart Ehrman, but through blockbuster novels like *The Da Vinci Code* and the hit action movie *The Matrix*.

Better known, perhaps, but not widely understood.

Alternative Christianities are "alternative" only because other, competing forms of Christianity rose to dominance. As a historian I often wonder what the world would have looked like if one of these now-vanished forms of Christianity had assumed the mantle of orthodoxy—or if Christianity had remained as pluralistic as it was when it began. Imagine for a moment that Gnostic Christianity had survived this early process of natural selection and that what we now call orthodox Christianity had become extinct.

You are a devout Gnostic Christian who has just moved to a new city. In the parish you moved away from, you participated in a Gnostic spiritual group that eagerly devoted itself to Bible study, prayer, and meditation, both solitary and communal; you also engaged in intense theological and spiritual debate. You and the members of your spiritual group expected far more out of church than what could be garnered from a Sunday morning worship service and coffee hour.

You believe in the superiority of the spiritual world; you distrust the material, created world. You believe that the Bible provides instructions for an ascent out of the material world and into God's realm—and the Bible you study includes books that don't appear in Catholic or Protestant Bibles today, such as the *Gospel of Thomas,* the *Gospel of Mary,* and the *Apocryphon of John.* You log on to the Internet to find a similar church in this new city.

The Sethian Gnostics come up first. Their version of Christianity seems quite compatible with what you are used to. The whole community functions like your old Gnostic study group: almost everyone meditates and most attend meditation services at the church; they pray ecstatically; and they have a really incredible intellectual life. They study the stars and find deep, hidden meanings in the most familiar of Bible passages. You never know what new twist they'll give to the liturgy.

But when you look at other options, the Valentinians seem very promising, too. They advertise, however, that the service for the coming Sunday is only for the most spiritual members of their community. As a non-initiate you would not be welcome. You make a mental note to see if they offer catechesis (instruction in the tenets of their spiritual system). Perhaps when you have some time you can audit one of their classes.

The Encratite Christians sound intriguing. Though not Gnostics, they have a lot in common with them. Encratite means "self-controlled" or "self-regulating," and these Christians not only engage in punishing fasts and intense prayer but reject marriage and sex because they believe salvation is available only to the bodily pure. But your spouse might not be thrilled at the prospect of your joining this group, so you scroll down to the fourth option.

The Marcionites are not really Gnostics, either, but they have always intrigued you. Like you, they distinguish between two Gods, one the evil creator of the material universe and the other the loving spiritual God who is the father of Jesus. What is strange to you, however, is that they have deleted every reference to the lesser creator God from their scriptures. They do not acknowledge the Old Testament at all, nor do they include the Gospels of Matthew, Mark, and John in their canon. It would be interesting to hear from them. The Net tells you that their bishop will be preaching next Sunday; this might be a good time to find out what else Marcionite Christianity has to offer. Your search completed, you are heartened to know that your city has such a generous selection of Christianities from which you can choose.

This fantasy gives a sense of what the possibilities might have been if orthodox Christianity had not prevailed over all other kinds of Christianity. During the first centuries of Christianity, Gnostic, Sethian, Valentinian, Marcionite, and Encratite churches thrived alongside orthodox churches that claimed Peter, James, John, or some other apostle as their founder. Christianity was not one religion but many, brimming with wildly divergent beliefs, extravagantly different styles of worship, and theologies that both challenged and delighted the mind.

Christianity is similarly diverse today—there are Catholic, Orthodox, and Protestant churches, and innumerable denominations along the way. Presbyterians and Episcopalians, Russian Orthodox and Roman Catholics, Methodists and Southern Baptists use different liturgies and offer radically different perspectives on some major theological issues—but few today question whether or not they are all really Christian. The early varieties of Christianity that will be discussed in this book were condemned as heresies; those who considered themselves orthodox sought to stamp them out. Eventually they succeeded—if these divergent ideas couldn't be extirpated altogether (Gnosticism returned with a vengeance at the beginning of the second millennium with the Cathar heresy, for example; the Reformation revived some of the earliest challenges to orthodox Christianity), all of these groups were exiled from the church and eventually disappeared.

THE INVENTION OF ORTHODOXY

Obviously this is not the story that most Christians learn in Sunday school, where they are taught that "orthodox" Christianity is the religion that Jesus founded, and these lost varieties, if they are mentioned at all, are dismissed as deviations from or corruptions of the original model. Why do we believe this myth?

Part of the reason goes back to the Roman emperor Constantine. In 325 C.E., the church was embroiled in a controversy about the nature of Christ. Followers of Arius (ca. 250–336 C.E.), a Libyan-born priest who had been a deacon in Alexandria, believed that Jesus was not of the same substance as his Father but had been created by him—in other words, that there was a time when Jesus had not yet existed. Bishop Alexander of

---

Why B.C.E. or C.E.?

B.C.E. stands for "Before the Common Era," as opposed to B.C., which means "Before Christ." C.E. stands for "the Common Era" and replaces A.D., which is the abbreviation for the Latin term *anno Domini,* "Year of the Lord." The new designations intentionally avoid dating people and events by reference to Jesus Christ in order to allow people of other faiths to use a common dating system without religious prejudice. It is also important for Christians because the dating of the life of Christ has been adjusted to account for errors in tabulating the years that were made during the Middle Ages. According to the corrected calendar Jesus was born in 4 B.C.E. and died in 29 C.E., which renders B.C. and A.D. meaningless.

Alexandria condemned the notion as heretical and removed Arius from his post, but the idea quickly spread throughout the Christian world. Possibly because of its intuitive appeal, the Arian heresy was particularly widespread and stubborn.

Constantine, the first Christian emperor, needed Christianity to be doctrinally consistent and centrally organized if it was going to help him hold together the vast empire he had inherited. Hoping to create a strong sense of unity and cohesion among his subjects, he summoned some three hundred bishops from Rome, Alexandria, Athens, Constantinople, Jerusalem, Italy, Greece, Arabia, Egypt, Syria, and Gaul to a meeting in the Turkish city of Nicaea. This first ecumenical council—so called because its participants represented the entire "inhabited world" (*oecumene* in Greek)—formulated a credo, a pledge that all Christians could recite that affirmed their basic beliefs. Along with this Nicene Creed came a revisionist account of Christian history. According to the bishops, Christianity originated in Jesus' teachings, which were then spread by his male disciples—first to the Jews, and then through Paul to the Gentiles. The bishops derived their authority from the Catholic (or "universal") Church, which was founded by the apostles. It was a monolithic, unidimensional description of how the church came to be.

Constantine's plan did not succeed, of course. Unity cannot be willed. But by attempting to draw a straight line from Jesus to themselves as Jesus' representatives and successors on earth, and reviling any deviations from this path as heresy, the bishops of the Nicene Council excluded many alternative forms of Christianity. The word "heretic" comes from the Greek word meaning "to choose for one's self." Those who went their own way, thinking different thoughts from the bishops, living lives

Text of the Nicene Creed

We believe in one God, the Father, the Almighty, creator of everything seen and unseen. We believe in one Lord Jesus Christ, the son of God, the only begotten of his Father, that is of the essence of the Father; God from true God, begotten, not made, being of one substance with the Father through whom all things were made, things in heaven and on the earth. For us humans and for our salvation, he came down, and he became enfleshed, and he became human, he suffered, and he rose again on the third day, and he went up to the heavens, and he will come again to judge the living and the dead.

And [we believe in] the Holy Spirit.

As for those who say "there was a time when he was not," and "before he was begotten he did not exist," or that "he was fabricated from another substance or nature," or that "the son of God is changeable or differentiated," these the holy Catholic Church anathematizes.

a little on the edge, maybe looking peculiar or sounding a little too intellectually elitist to bishops' ears—those are the ones the emperor and the bishops drove off. Too bad. The surviving church lost some really interesting people.

The hunt for heretics didn't begin with the Nicene Council. Irenaeus (ca. 130–202), the bishop of Lyons in Gaul, first stepped up to the plate, setting the tone for every subsequent heresy hunter. His cantankerous attitude toward the Gnostics and other alternative Christianities, as well as the sniping and disdainful tone of his writings, left no doubt that he was in charge. But before he could launch his attacks on the alternative Christians, Irenaeus had to create an alternative Christianity of his own—one that we now call "orthodox Christianity."

What Is Orthodoxy?

"Orthodoxy" is hard to define. The easiest way to understand it is that it is what remains of Christianity after all its heresies have been removed. Various ecumenical councils of the church decided what was and wasn't heretical; the positive articulation of doctrines (such as the person of Christ, the Trinity, the Creeds) almost all came in reaction to some unorthodox thinking or practice that was being condemned. Orthodoxy may also refer to those churches that are in communion with the ancient bishops of Rome, Alexandria, Constantinople, or Antioch (in Syria), who led most of the early ecumenical councils.

THE "BIG BANG" THEORY OF CHRISTIAN ORIGINS
After the Council of Nicaea, the imperially sanctioned and militarily supported separation of Christians into two camps, heretical and orthodox, began. Prior to that time, Christianity had gone off in a number of different directions simultaneously. This diversity of beliefs goes all the way back to the earliest days of Christianity—to the time of Jesus himself.

I subscribe to what I might call, using an analogy from physics, the "big bang" theory of Christian origins. This theory begins not with the bishops' stories but with the study of Christian literature in its historical and chronological sequence.

If we look at New Testament writings in their chronological order, this diversity becomes self-evident. Chronologically, Paul's letters—rather than any words of Jesus—provide the earliest evidence for Christianity.

Paul's earliest letter (First Thessalonians) was written sometime in 50 c.e., approximately twenty years after the crucifixion of Jesus. In contrast, the earliest gospel, the Gospel of Mark, was composed sometime between 65 and 70 c.e., some thirty-five to forty years after the crucifixion. Matthew (written ca. 90) and Luke (written ca. 100) used Mark's gospel as a starting point, but significantly revised it for their own particular communities. The author of John wrote his gospel about 110 c.e., giving an interpretation of Jesus' life and works that was altogether different from his predecessors'. Each author drew as well on collections of Jesus' sayings and other sources, which offered up different accounts of the same events and altogether unique stories.

Even this brief chronology shows how diverse Christianity was at its very beginning. Each community of believers used the materials it inherited to develop its own story about Jesus. Each community reworked the tradition to address particular issues that spoke to its own circumstances. No monolith here. The "big bang," an explosion of diverse Christianities, was woven into the very fabric of the New Testament.

In the end, Constantine and the bishops couldn't wipe out the alternative Christianities that they had competed with for so long. They stood too close to the heart of Christianity to be driven out without killing Christianity itself. Alternative and orthodox Christianities were closely bound, if not chained, to one another; they compelled each other to articulate clearly what they believed and how they differed. In fact, the bishops' story of "orthodox" Christianity makes scant sense unless you know the "heretical" ideas they were reacting to. Christian diversity lived on for centuries, and it is reemerging in our own era. That diversity is what this book is about.

Here you will read about Gnostics, intellectuals, ascetics, and charismatics. There were Sethians and Valentinians, Marcionites, Encratites, and Montanists—all of them inheritors of the scriptures, all of them claiming a deep and abiding relationship to Jesus and the Kingdom of God he proclaimed. You will learn about unfamiliar gospels—by Mary, Thomas, Philip, and others—that taught different, challenging, and fascinating theologies and expressed new ways of experiencing the Christian God. Finally, you will learn about some of Christianity's strongest competitors from outside the faith—the Manicheans and the Neoplatonists.

Over the course of its history, Christianity has learned how to incorporate different understandings, practices, and beliefs under one umbrella. The Protestant Reformation undermined the monolithic story that the bishops had tried to impose for so long; alternative Christianities are now accepted as legitimate denominations. The fantasy with which I began this book may not be so outlandish as it seems. The various forms of contemporary Christianity often reflect the same issues, the same modes of thinking, or similar conclusions about holiness, the world, and the way to salvation that we find in early Christianity. But before we can make those connections, we need to know where that diversity began.

Note: Except where other translators are noted, all of the translations that appear in this volume are my own.

TIMELINE: A CHRONOLOGY OF
EARLY CHRISTIAN HISTORY
AND LITERATURE

4 B.C.E.–29 C.E.: Jesus' life

35 C.E.: Paul embraces his mission to include the Gentiles

35–38: Paul's missionary activity in Arabia (Gal 1:17)

38: Paul visits with Peter in Jerusalem (Gal 1:18)

38–48: Paul's missionary activity in Cilicia and Syria (Gal 1:21)

Collections of the Sayings of Jesus (until about 50 C.E.)

Early sayings of the *Gospel of Thomas*

Sayings collected in the Synoptic Sayings Source for Matthew and Luke

Collections of miracles (until about 55 C.E.)

The miracle collections of Mark and the Signs Source of John

Healing stories in the Hellenistic mode (missionary competition)

Apocalyptic scenarios (Paul's letters, Mark 13, and others)

48: Apostolic Council in Jerusalem (Gal 2:1ff.; Acts 15)

48 OR 49: Paul's "incident" with Peter at Antioch (Gal 2:11ff.)

50: Paul's 1 Thessalonians

52: Paul's Letter to the Galatians

52: Paul's 1 Corinthians and the letter preserved in 2 Cor 2:14–6:13; 7:2–4

54–55: Paul's Letter to the Philippians, Philemon, and 2 Cor 10–13

55: Paul's letter preserved in 2 Cor 1:1–2:13; 7:5–16

55–56: Paul's Letter to the Romans

56: Paul travels to Jerusalem; the collection; his imprisonment

56–58: Paul's imprisonment in Caesarea

58: Paul travels to Rome

60: Paul's martyrdom

66–70: The Jewish uprising

65–70: The Gospel of Mark; the beginnings of rabbinic Judaism

66: Fighting erupts in Palestine

67: The emperor Nero appoints Vespasian to suppress the Jewish revolt

68: Vespasian proclaimed emperor while in Palestine

68: Titus appointed to Palestine to suppress revolt

70: Titus destroys the Temple in Jerusalem and takes the spoils to Rome

80: Pauline school's Letter to the Colossians

90: The Gospel of Matthew

95: Letter to the Ephesians (as cover letter to the publication of the Pauline letters)

100: The Gospel of Luke (Volume 1 of the Luke/Acts work)

100: The Revelation of John

100–110: The Gospel of John; Johannine letters (1 John; 2 John; 3 John)

110: 1 Peter

110: The *Gospel of Thomas*

115: Acts of the Apostles (Volume 2 of the Luke/Acts work)

125: The Pastoral Epistles (1 Timothy; 2 Timothy; Titus) and the *Acts of Paul and Thecla*

125: Epistle to the Hebrews

125: Letter to Jude

130: 2 Peter, James

132–135: The uprising of Simon Bar Kochba; Hadrian renames Jerusalem Aelia Capitolina

150–155: Marcion; Valentinus

THE MANY KINGDOMS OF GOD

Everyone who "comes in the Name of the Lord" ought to be received, but later when you have examined him you will know him, for you have the comprehension of the good and the bad. If the one who comes is a traveler, help him as much as you are able, but he will not stay with you more than two days, or perhaps three if needs be.

—THE *DIDACHE* XII.1–2

JESUS AND DIVERSITY

Diversity in Christianity came directly from Jesus himself. It began long before his death, with the first proclamations of the Kingdom of God. This aspect of earliest Christianity—its multifacetedness, its inclusion of radically different conceptions of itself—was buried by the triumphalist story that the bishops wrote after they'd successfully suppressed their rivals. It will take some digging to uncover it but it is worth the effort. We will need to put aside some of our preconceptions before we can understand Jesus' mission and why he *encouraged* such diverse understandings of the religion he ended up founding.

First of all, Jesus was not a Christian. Jesus was a Jew who lived in a region occupied by the Romans. There two very different cultures and religious orientations thrived side by side, the Roman and the Jewish. The region was probably trilingual: Greek, spoken by all; Aramaic, spoken by the local people of Palestine and Judea; and Latin, the official administrative language of the Roman occupation forces. Jesus probably spoke two of these languages. We presume he spoke Greek because all of his preserved sayings—and in fact all of the earliest surviving Christian literature—exist primarily in Greek. Greek was the common language of the peoples living in occupied Judea, and it had been the intellectual language of the Jews since the time of Alexander the Great three centuries before. It is virtually certain that Jesus spoke Aramaic since it was the common language of the indigenous peoples of his region.

Second, Jesus never said he was God. I know this is hard for many contemporary Christians to understand, but it is true nonetheless. Christians affirm that Jesus *is* God, but that is something that Christians say, not anything that Jesus ever said about himself.

Jesus focused on proclaiming the Kingdom of God, a divine empire under God's sole imperial authority. He never clearly defined his own role in that kingdom. He never even defined precisely what constituted the Kingdom. He just proclaimed it to anyone who understood Greek. In the Greek-speaking Roman world there were many ways of understanding the divine nature of a person. Roman emperors, for example, were made gods upon their death, making the living emperor a "son of God." Although Jews maintained a monotheistic theology, they also included divine figures, or at least semidivine characters, in their worldview. Sophia, the divine mind of God, whose name literally means "wisdom," was one such figure. Jesus would have appeared as a divine messenger to Romans by virtue of his proclamation of the Kingdom of God and to Jews as well by virtue of the divine wisdom that he spoke. But Jesus never declared himself divine.

Third, if Jesus preached in Greek as opposed to Aramaic, we have to assume that he intended to communicate with anyone who could understand the language—Gentile and Jew alike. Jesus' message was not delivered just to the Jews and then carried to the Gentiles by Paul after his death, as most of our histories of Christianity tell us. Jesus intentionally undertook a universal mission himself. The use of Greek as the primary language of the proclamation of Jesus and the proclamation of the Kingdom of God by Jesus' followers emphasizes the universal mission of early Christianity. It is because this mission was *already* universal that Paul began his mission to the Gentiles. None of Paul's adversaries objected to his mission; they objected only to his dismissal of Jewish religious rites and practices for the Gentile Christians. The early church understood Paul's mission to be a continuation of Jesus' own.

Fourth, Jesus told people to enter the Kingdom of God and to create it in their own contexts. He said such things as "the Kingdom of God is close to you!" (Luke 10:9), and "the Kingdom of God is within you" (Luke 17:21), and "blessed are the poor because the Kingdom of God is yours" (Luke 6:20). And of course Jesus often introduced his parables with "the Kingdom of God is like . . . " followed by a story. The Kingdom of God was his message. The Kingdom of God, however, did not look like any other kingdom of the world. You might say it looked like the opposite. The poor, the meek, and the hungry became leaders in that kingdom. When abused, the members of the Kingdom turned the other cheek. They did not expect to earn any interest on money loaned or even to have the money returned. Jesus proclaimed a really remarkable Kingdom of God that turned everything on its head. He proclaimed it both to Gentiles and to Jews, and he proclaimed it in Greek so that everyone could understand. Of course, there were some, like James, John, and Peter, Mary Magdalene, and Jesus' mother Mary, who knew Jesus personally during his lifetime. But realistically, most of Jesus' early followers probably knew him only by reputation, by hearing some report about Jesus' words or deeds, or by a kind of mystical experience of the Kingdom Jesus proclaimed. But all of them sought to extend the Kingdom of God as they understood it and gather all the peoples of the world into it. The Kingdom and the people who proclaimed it spread like wildfire.

These earliest Kingdom movements remained as diverse as the people who proclaimed them. We can see this in the Epistles of Paul. Some movements followed Jewish law as it was given in the Old Testament while others rejected it. Some movements insisted that men be circumcised; others rejected the custom. Some claimed to perform miracles; others rejected the possibility. Some devoted themselves to understanding the revelation in the Old Testament; others lived out their lives guided only by God's spirit.

Most of these communities, however, differed starkly in one way from Jesus' own preaching. They recognized him as God's own Son, not just as a divine messenger, but as a divinity in his own right. Their proclamation of Jesus as God's Son and the savior of the world through his death and resurrection nevertheless resulted in a multiplicity of beliefs and practices. The New Testament attests to that great diversity; indeed, it preserved in its own pages many of the conflicts and arguments about what was central to the faith.

MULTICULTURAL PAUL

Paul's letters provide a window into the conflictual diversity of early Christianity. By examining his relationship with other Christian missionaries we can uncover the roots of some of the lost Christianities. Almost every one of his letters begins with his self-designation as "Paul, an apostle of Jesus Christ." Paul differed from the other apostles in that they had known Jesus personally, whereas Paul knew him only spiritually. Sometime after the crucifixion, Paul had a vision of Jesus that was so powerful that he not only became Jesus' follower but took himself to Arabia and Syria to tell non-Jews, the Gentiles, about the Kingdom of God that Jesus proclaimed. Furthermore, he declared that these non-Jews needn't follow Jewish law to enter the Kingdom of God. No need for consulting with anyone. He just did it. The vision was enough!

Paul tells us this story in his letter to the Galatians (1:11–2:14). But he also tells us how, fifteen years later, he ran afoul of other missionaries in the Jesus movements. Paul decided to go to Jerusalem to confer with James, John, and Peter, the acknowledged pillars of the church. At first, the meeting didn't go well—the disciples were adamant that to be a Christian you had to follow Jewish law: circumcision, dietary rules, all the laws of the Old Testament.

Paul was outraged by this imposition on Gentile believers, for Jesus had revealed something different to him. Yes,

Jesus had sent him to the Gentiles to bring them into Israel's inheritance—but that did not include the law. The law was appropriate for Jews, but Gentiles could enter the Kingdom through faith in Jesus alone. Here were two radically different understandings of the Christian life—and both of them are found in the Christian scriptures.

At last the apostles compromised, agreeing that the only law Paul and his churches needed to obey was to remember the poor (Galatians 2:10), which Paul was eager to do anyway. They sent Paul on his way. At first everything went as well as could be expected among people who disagreed so seriously.

But as Paul tells us, it turned out to be an uneasy compromise. Paul started off toward Asia Minor and Greece to build churches among the Gentiles. The Jerusalem apostles had hoped that these two kinds of Christianity, Jewish and Gentile, could coexist. But almost immediately there was friction. While Peter was on his own mission to the Jews of Antioch he visited one of the churches that Paul was founding among the Gentiles. Peter and Paul found themselves at a mixed dinner party of Jews and Gentiles, all followers of Jesus and members of the Kingdom of God. Paul was delighted: to his mind, this was precisely what Jesus wanted—Jews and Gentiles eating together at the same table. But Peter couldn't bring himself to violate the Jewish dietary law. Yes, Gentiles and Jews could eat together, he said—provided that the Gentiles first adopted Jewish customs. Peter withdrew and a furious Paul confronted him face to face; they parted less than friends. The contour of the perpetual argument within Christianity between unity and diversity had been set.

Paul's troubles did not end there. His opponents and enemies dogged his tracks, attempting to undo his work in the churches he had already founded. Paul complained about these rival Christian missionaries in 2 Corinthians. Two groups were particularly inimical.

About the first group, Paul says, "I'm not like those others, the peddlers of God's Word!" (2:11). These so-called "peddlers" came with letters of recommendation from other cities. A letter of recommendation was a meal ticket—one person writes another to commend a person for free room and board, or some other material assistance. These traveling-salesman-type evangelists lived well while they preached the gospel; in contrast, Paul complained that he had to work with his own hands to support himself. Paul did not argue with their message but with their methods. He valued self-sufficiency; they valued the good life. They brought letters of recommendation to get provision; Paul wrote his own letter of recommendation on the hearts of the Corinthian believers. Moreover, these rival evangelists embarrassed and humiliated Paul, saying that he did not deserve to be supported, impugning both his person and his message.

The second group was even more vicious than the first. Paul referred to them mockingly as those "superlative apostles" (12:11), but he had to fight fiercely to hold on to the Corinthians he had converted. These superlative apostles claimed that while Paul's letters were powerful, his personal presence was weak and contemptible (10:10). They told the Corinthians that Paul's letters were aimed at terrifying them. Infuriated, Paul countered that his adversaries preached a different Jesus; they had a different spirit; they proclaimed a different gospel. History has not preserved the exact content of his rivals' teachings, but we can surmise by Paul's defense of himself that the gospel they proclaimed was more oriented to Jewish practice: they announced themselves as Hebrews and Israelites (11:22); they boasted of special visions and revelations (12:1–5); they performed miraculous deeds (12:12). Paul insisted that he was all of those, too—he was a Hebrew, he had received visions, and he knew Jesus. Eventually the Corinthians reconciled with Paul, but he had a hard time. Some of 2 Corinthians reads like testimony from a painful divorce trial.

Paul's letters indicate just the tip of the iceberg of early Christian diversity, a state of affairs that would eventually drive the bishops to distraction and, a few centuries later, impel the first Christian emperor to the use of force to establish and maintain uniform belief and practice. They provide a record of the vigorous competition between the early evangelists, their profound disagreements about what is true and important, and the violent emotions inspired by their theological positions—all in all, of the incredible variety of expression that characterized Christianity in its earliest years.

THE VARIETIES OF GNOSTIC EXPERIENCE

Wisdom is radiant and unfading, and she is easily discerned by those who love her, and is found by those who seek her. She hastens to make herself known to those who desire her. One who rises early to seek her will have no difficulty, for she will be found sitting at the gate. To fix one's thought on her is perfect understanding, and one who is vigilant on her account will soon be free of care, because she goes about seeking those worthy of her, and she graciously appears to them in their paths, and meets them in every thought.

—WISDOM OF SOLOMON 6:12–15
NEW REVISED STANDARD VERSION

BURIED TREASURE

Gnostics have so often been caricatured throughout the course of Western history that it is difficult for us to envision them as real, living, serious-minded people. Actually they are not as strange as the popular imagination has made them out to be; they were simply religious enthusiasts with an intellectual bent and an intense spirituality. Gnosticism was subtle, sophisticated, and audacious; it dazzled the mind. Gnostics of every variety thought of themselves as a spiritually vital, intellectually curious religious elite.

Gnosticism made the conventional church look drab and boring, almost stupid in comparison. This dismayed the bishops, who did not appreciate being characterized as the leaders of a flock of dullards and the spiritually lax. So the church's opposition to Gnosticism began early and stayed late, starting in the second century and continuing right up until the present day.

The biggest difficulty with studying Gnosticism is that until very recently it was defined exclusively by its opponents. Most of what we know about it comes from arguments against it, written by its enemies in the second, third, and fourth centuries. Irenaeus (130–200) and Tertullian (160–240), Hippolytus (170–236), and Epiphanius (310–403) were its most prominent critics. Even the non-Christian Plotinus (205–269), a third-century Neoplatonist philosopher, took a shot at it. It seems that the Gnostics were threatening to everyone. Their opponents made them look like comic book villains, accusing them of everything from stupidity to incest and cannibalism. This relentlessly one-sided vision of Gnosticism might have remained unchallenged had it not been for a remarkable discovery in Egypt.

One day in 1945, an Egyptian youth named Muhammad Ali al-Samman and his brothers rode their camels out to the Jabal al Tarif, a huge cliff across the Nile River from the town of Nag Hammadi, to dig for *sabakh*, a soft, nitrogen-rich soil that they used for fertilizer. When they uncovered a large red earthenware jar, they wondered if it didn't contain a jinn, a spirit. But they had heard legends that gold was buried in the caves that dotted the cliff, so they broke it open.

They were disappointed—all they found in the jar were

some old codices (books written on papyrus). They brought them back to their house and left them near the oven. Their mother put the books to practical use, tearing pages out of them and using them as kindling for her fires, but eventually—while the police were questioning the brothers about a murder they'd committed in a blood feud—the books were entrusted to a local priest for safekeeping. After a long, fraught journey through the black market, they came into the hands of scholars, who identified them as Coptic translations of long-lost Gnostic texts that had originally been written in Greek: the *Gospel of Thomas*, the *Gospel of Philip*, the *Apocryphon of John*, the *First and Second Apocalypse of James*, the *Gospel of Truth*, *On the Origin of the World*, the *Sophia of Jesus Christ*, and many more. Most likely a monk whose bishop had forbidden him to read unsanctioned books had hidden them in the late fourth century. Now that they had been miraculously recovered, for the first time we could hear the Gnostics in their own voices, not mediated through the distorted, parodic paraphrases of their opponents.

One point still needs to be made. For the most part, *gnosis* had a positive connotation in the early days of the church. Clement of Alexandria (ca. 150–215), a significant second-century Christian theologian, used the term "true Gnostic" as a legitimate category for understanding the Christian life, and no one questions his orthodoxy. Clement's kind of Gnostic was fine, but others were not. Even Irenaeus distinguished between true and "falsely so-called *gnosis*" in his compendium of heresies. The opposing bishops made sure we knew the difference between true knowledge, which they taught, and the false knowledge taught by the Gnostics they opposed.

Very few people in antiquity actually called themselves Gnostics. Many philosophers, Jewish biblical interpreters, and Christian apostles and teachers, as well as adherents of other ancient religions such as the Hermeticists (see chapter 8), used the term *"gnosis,"* the Greek word meaning knowledge, to refer to a wide assortment of things. The term "Gnosticism" itself does not appear in ancient texts; it is only since the mid-eighteenth century that scholars have used the designation as a convenient means of unifying the complex and variegated movements oriented toward *gnosis.*

WHAT IS A GNOSTIC?

More than knowledge, *gnosis* connotes understanding, intuitive perception, insight, learning. In the most general terms, Gnostics are simply those who are oriented toward knowledge and understanding—or perception and learning—as a particular modality for living. More specifically, Gnosticism refers to the various associations and movements founded in the first centuries of the Common Era (though varieties of Gnosticism have emerged in every age) by those who called themselves Gnostics—or, more important, whom others characterized as such.

In every generation there are some people who simply cannot accept or find much satisfaction in the standard answers to the ultimate questions of human existence. They want something more, for themselves and for their coreligionists, than what they perceive to be the lowest level of understanding, so that they might know the best and most fulfilling way to live.

Seeking a greater depth of understanding, the Gnostics investigate and pursue religion in the light of the most complex and richly variegated intellectual tradition of their day. They analyze what constitutes proper social relationships, in order to create profoundly cohesive associations of people with similar intellectual and spiritual interests. They embrace current science and seek to understand the connection between the physical and the spiritual realms. Gnostics doggedly pursue the very knowledge that others seem not to grasp, a knowledge that draws them from the safety of known categories and ideas to the insecurity of religious and spiritual questing.

This description of Gnosticism underscores its elite mentality. Gnostics pride themselves on having access to information that's not for the consumption of the general public but reserved only for those few who are capable of study and understanding (esoteric, as opposed to exoteric, knowledge). Gnostics, in short, represent seekers of a particularly intellectual and spiritual sort. We have all known the type.

Gnostics know that the world they experience on a day-to-day level is illusory and wicked. In the movie *The Matrix,* the hero discovers that the world he thought he lived in—a present-day American city—is actually an illusion created by an evil intelligence who wishes to keep humans asleep and thus enslaved; in another movie, *The Truman Show,* the hapless protagonist discovers that the only world he has ever known is a stage set—that everyone and everything he's ever cared about are false and that the god of his world, the director of the TV show that he has unknowingly starred in for all of his life, has deliberately kept him in ignorance of his true nature. The popularity of the paranoid science fiction of Philip K. Dick (his novels provided the plots for such popular movies as *Minority Report, Blade Runner,* and *Total Recall*) and the seemingly irresistible appeal of *X-Files* conspiracy-mongering about everything from UFOs to the Kennedy assassination and the origins of AIDS suggest that this suspicion—that "reality" is not what it seems, that malicious powers are deliberately lying to us—is hard-wired into the human brain. If Gnostic religion is rare nowadays, Gnostic beliefs and attitudes are not.

As with most religious movements, the Gnostic sects of the early Christian era have a few things in common, but more things differentiate and contrast them. Later chapters will explore specific Gnostic traditions, movements, beliefs, and practices. But here let me outline the commonalities among the different versions of Christian Gnosticism, based on my wide reading in both the ancient texts about the writings of heretics and the newly discovered Gnostic literature.

But first we should ask a basic question: Where did these early Christian Gnostics come from?

It is an interesting and unsolvable problem. Scholars have argued about it for centuries. All agree that Gnosticism was a product of cultural and intellectual clashes. Did it emerge in the pre-Christian era when Persian dualism, a belief in the strict separation of light and darkness or good and evil, and the monotheistic Israelite religion, a belief in the one true God of Israel, were at odds with each other? If yes, this would make Gnosticism a very old religion. Or was Gnosticism entirely a dualistic Persian import to the West? Also ancient. Perhaps Gnosticism was a product of the clash between the Hellenistic Greek culture put in place by Alexander the Great and his followers throughout the Middle East and a newly emerging

Christianity, what the influential scholar Adolf von Harnack called the "acute Hellenization of Christianity"? Certainly Gnosticism and Christianity coexisted for many years. Possibly Gnosticism first arose among the Jews, as a theological response to the traumas they suffered during the Jewish wars with the Romans. Since all of Gnosticism seems to be particularly interested in what the first few chapters of Genesis said about the creation of the world and human beings, this makes intuitive sense. But still other scholars say no, Gnosticism arose primarily as a Christian movement that broke away from orthodox Christianity.

All of these theories are plausible; no one can prove or disprove any one of them beyond the shadow of a doubt. We simply do not know where Gnosticism came from or what caused it to become so popular. But popular it was: if we can believe the reports of the heresy hunters, it penetrated to every corner of the ancient Christian world.

WHAT DID THE CHRISTIAN GNOSTICS BELIEVE?

A Gnostic of the first five centuries of the Common Era felt imprisoned by his or her body and by the physical world, which prevented the exploration of true insight and knowledge, or *gnosis*, that the Gnostic so avidly desired. The body and the physical world were problems to be solved: material existence, whether of the self or of the cosmos, was by nature bad.

This belief, this problem of the body and material existence, emerged from a particular understanding of the relationship between the spiritual and the material worlds. Gnostics understood these worlds to be separate and divided: the material world was a place of entrapment, the spiritual world afforded liberation. The Gnostic myth of creation describes the origins of this dualism.

Gnostics believed that an evil demiurge—the term they used to describe the fabricator of the physical universe—created the material world and the bodies that inhabit it. The true spiritual God—another deity altogether—created the spiritual world and the spiritual bodies of humans. The demiurge, who opposed the true God, probably out of ignorance and arrogance, entrapped people in their bodies and within the material world to prevent them from attaining the purely spiritual and immaterial world that was created by the true God. This problem of materiality and its deleterious effect on the human pursuit of reality was the foundation of all Gnostic systems.

The Greek word *demiourgos* (which literally means "artisan") had some stature in Platonic philosophy, notably Plato's *Timaeus,* in which it characterized and referred to the fabricator of all material creation. The ancients assumed the preexistence of matter prior to the creation of the world, so the demiurge used material already available to create the world and the humans who lived in it. In Platonic philosophy, this was an entirely positive process.

The Jews and the Christians, however, could not use this term to describe a God who created the world out of nothing (ex nihilo), as described in Genesis. The Jewish and the orthodox Christian God did two things: first God brought being out of nothingness; and second, God created both the material and the spiritual worlds—in other words, the creator God and the demiurgic God of Gnosticism were one and the same. However, while the Gnostics valued and appreciated the world of the spiritual creator God, they believed that the demiurge had fabricated the material world precisely to prevent humans from understanding and knowing the true creator God. The physical world was a trap that caused a seeming narcosis, or a sleep state, among humans. *Gnosis,* true knowledge and insight, began when the stupor induced by the demiurge was overcome.

That awakening required a savior who would come to release the Gnostics from their stupor of materiality. The savior's work was to proclaim the existence of the spiritual world and the reality of the true, spiritual God. This proclamation was a clarion call to throw off the dulling effects of material existence and to begin to pursue the way to true, spiritual knowledge.

HIDDEN KNOWLEDGE—THE KEY
THAT UNLOCKS THE SPIRIT

But how to do this? How could the Gnostics transcend their materiality and ascend to the higher, more spiritual world? The demiurge locked their true spiritual selves behind the door of materiality. Once the Gnostics had the proper key to unlock that door, they could enter the truly spiritual world. The key was *gnosis,* secret and mysterious knowledge.

But what was this hidden knowledge? Each Gnostic system answered that question in different ways, as we will see in subsequent chapters, but I can provide a general characterization here. That knowledge consisted first of all in the recognition that the material world and embodied existence prevented Gnostics from knowing their true selves and their true and spiritual God. True knowledge was deposited in the sacred scriptures, the Bible. So much of Gnostic knowledge emerged from the interpretation of specific biblical passages: in the Old Testament, the creation of the world and of the first human being in Genesis 1:26–28 and especially the second creation story of Genesis 2:4–3:24; the killing of Cain by Abel (Genesis 4:1–15); and the stories about Seth (Genesis 4:25); in the New Testament, the story of the mustard seed (Luke 13:18–19; Matthew 13:31–32) and the parable of the workers for the harvest (Matthew 20:1–16). When properly interpreted, these biblical passages (and many others as well) provided the Gnostic with the saving knowledge that would thwart the demiurge.

That knowledge also involved the recognition that the mind needed to be awakened from its material stupor before it could be connected to the truly spiritual world and to the divine mind that created it. Theological anthropology, the religious understanding of the nature of the human being, provided the rationale. Human beings consisted of body, soul (*psyche*), and spirit (*pneuma*). Gnostics believed that only the spirit, not the soul, could intuit the divine realm. Therefore, the body needed to be trained to submit to the soul, and the soul, in turn, to submit to the spirit, which connected the human to God. Gnostics often described this process as discovering and following a "divine spark" that resided in the person, a divine spirit that, properly understood, would lead to true knowledge of self and of the true God.

To defeat the demiurge and gain access to the divine mind of God, Gnostics also required up-to-date "scientific" knowledge, which they gleaned from cosmology, astrology, demonology, angelology, medicine, physics, mathematics, geometry, and sophisticated interpretations of the scriptures (remember, the "scientific method," with its objective proofs and experimentation, was still more than a thousand years in the future. Much of what the Gnostics considered scientific, we would classify as metaphysical). These scientific theories frequently colored Gnostic speculation. The cosmology of the day, for example, maintained that the physical world was characterized by dense materiality, but that the cosmic spheres became more and more spiritual in substance as they moved outward toward God. Gnostics applied their knowledge of the physical universe and the planets to help them advance from the physical world and into the ethereal realms of the spheres.

The Gnostics knew that good and evil supernatural entities regulated the human body. From their studies of angelology and demonology, Gnostics learned how to manipulate these beings in order to release the body from its material limitations. Much of their literature includes various incantations of divine letters, magical spells, secret names, and other mysterious phrases to assist in this endeavor.

All of this knowledge remained out of the reach of the normal person; it was available only to those select few who could hear the savior's call—and had the intellectual and spiritual insight to respond to it. The Gnostics thought of themselves as a select or elect people who had knowledge of the divine spark planted deep within them and who could follow it from their body through the entire cosmos to a mystical union with God.

The knowledge sought by these intensely intellectual seekers constituted a kind of doctoral-level education in the things of the spirit while the rest of humanity remained stuck in elementary school. Gnostics believed that only they had access to this elite knowledge. Only they understood the nature and goal of human existence. Only they knew where they came from and where they were going.

As for those ignorant unfortunates who were oriented only to the body and the soul, not to the divine spirit, many of them found much to resent in the Gnostics' smug sense of election. Resentment of the Gnostics' seemingly arrogant presumption, as much as any doctrinal issues, fueled the intense opposition that would eventually drive them underground.

Often these themes of the Gnostic call, the spark of knowledge, and the Gnostic election coalesce in Gnostic sayings. The following saying from the *Gospel of Thomas* reads almost like a Gnostic creed:

> Jesus said, "If interested people say to you, 'From where do you come?' reply to them, 'We come from the light, from the place where the light created itself, founded itself, and appeared in its own image.'
>
> "If they ask further, 'Are you the light?' reply to them, 'We are its children, and we are the elect of the living Father.'
>
> "If they ask you for proof that the Father dwells in you, answer them in this way, 'It is motion and rest.'"
>
> —*THE GOSPEL OF THOMAS*, SAYING 50

THE MYTH OF SOPHIA

Where did the demiurge come from? And what is the origin of this false, material universe that we are stuck in? The Gnostic myth of Sophia offers one answer. In some ancient Jewish traditions, Sophia (the Greek word for "wisdom") was represented not only as the personification of God's wisdom but as his consort. She appears in the so-called "wisdom books" of the Bible attributed to King Solomon—Ecclesiastes, Proverbs, and the Song of Songs. A reference to Sophia is also found in the peculiar plural used by God in the creation story, "Let *us* make man in our own image, according to our likeness" (Genesis 1:26). The plurals "us" and "our" are understood to refer to God and his consort, Wisdom.

In Gnostic tradition, Sophia was one of the spiritual beings that emanated from God. But whereas in Genesis God was the creator of the world, in Gnostic mythology Wisdom took the initiative and attempted to create the world without God's approval. Sophia's attempt was a failure—instead of a world, she created the demiurge, a hypostatization (a materialization) of her arrogant desire. The demiurge, in turn, created a world— our world—almost completely devoid of spirit and soul. Our only hope for redemption lies in the small divine spark from Sophia that found its way in.

Sophia's abortive creation disturbed the harmony of the divine realm, called the *pleroma* in Greek. *Pleroma* means fullness and completeness, which suggests perfection. In Gnostic cosmology, the cosmos consisted of eight planetary spheres, with the earth at their center. The ninth sphere was the divine realm. Progression through the spheres went from the most to the least material—and finally into the spiritual realm. This paralleled the life of the Gnostic who, through various kinds of knowledge, ascended to reunion with the divine realm by entering the ninth sphere, where God and all the divine beings dwelled. As they undertook their own journeys to salvation, Gnostics reversed the arrogant desire of Sophia and deconstructed the material world of the demiurge.

Ironically, it was Sophia's fall from divine grace that made possible the Gnostic ascent toward grace. As the Gnostic moved from the known material world to the unknown spiritual world, from the natural world to the supernatural world, from the imitation world of the demiurge to the true spiritual world of God, he or she retraced the steps of creation, back to their spiritual source. The material world was but a poor copy of the spiritual world—but it looked enough like its original to show the Gnostic the way back to truth and salvation.

Once in the spiritual world, the Gnostic would no longer be subject to birth or death. Being born and dying marked the material world as mutable, temporary, impermanent, and imperfect. The divine realm revolved about cycles of regeneration and renewal, the opposite of the material cycle.

Clement of Alexandria, the leading orthodox teacher of the famous Christian school in Alexandria, preserved some sayings of one of his contemporaries, a Gnostic teacher named Theodotus. In a passage that explains the basic tenets of Gnosticism, he writes:

> *Baptism alone does not save us.*
> *We are saved by the knowledge of who we are and where we began,*
> *where we have been and what we have become,*
> *where we are going and what has liberated us,*
> *what constitutes [real] birth and what constitutes [real] rebirth.*

—CLEMENT OF ALEXANDRIA, *EXCERPTS OF THEODOTUS* 78:2

Simply by knowing about the immutable world and initiating steps to advance toward it, the Gnostic made significant headway in his or her ascent.

GNOSTIC ANTHROPOLOGY

Gnostic philosophy divides the cosmos into different levels of purity and holiness—from the coarsest and most material to the finest and most spiritual. In the second century, a Gnostic teacher named Ptolemy wrote to an aristocratic Roman lady named Flora, urging her to join his group. In his letter, Ptolemy explained that the scriptures have three levels: the pure law of God, the law the Savior overthrew and rejected, and the symbolic law.

> *My dear sister Flora,*
>
> *Although the law was established through Moses, not many people have understood it properly. Most have an inaccurate knowledge both of the one who established it and of the law itself. . . .*
>
> *First, you should understand that the totality of the law in the Pentateuch of Moses was not instituted by only one legislator. I mean by this that some [of the Pentateuch] comes from God alone, some laws come from Moses, and still others come from other humans. The Savior's own words teach us this threefold attribution. The first part of the legislation ought to be ascribed only to God; the second part of the legislation ought to be ascribed to Moses, not in the sense that God spoke through Moses, but in the sense that Moses*

created some laws through his own thoughts; and the third part of
the law should be ascribed to the people's elders, who seem to have
created some of their own laws from the beginning. I can prove the
truth of this theory to you from the Savior's own teaching. . . .

The law of God, the first part I just mentioned, also has three
parts. The first contains pure commandments not polluted with
evil, which we properly call "the Law." The Savior came [as
Matthew 5:17 states] not to destroy this law but to fulfill it, for
the Savior was not an alien to the law but the law needed him
to complete it. On its own this law was not perfect yet. The second part of the law of God is mixed with inferior and unjust
thinking. The Savior came to destroy this part of the law because
it was foreign to the Savior's nature. The third part of the law
consists of material that is allegorical and symbolic. It presents an
image of transcendent spiritual realities. These the Savior
metaphorized, taking material from the physical and visible
world to refer to the invisible and spiritual world. . . .

So now you understand how the law of God is itself divided
into three parts. The Savior completed the first, for he includes
them in his prohibiting of anger, lust, and oath-taking the commandments: "You shall not kill. You shall not commit adultery.
You shall not swear falsely." The Savior completely destroyed the
second part: here the opposite replaces "An eye for an eye and a
tooth for a tooth," which is filled with injustice. The Savior opposed that old teaching with "For I say to you, do not resist the
evil person, but if anyone strikes you, turn the other cheek to
him." Finally, there is the law transformed and translated from
the literal meaning to the spiritual meaning. This law symboli-
cally represents spiritual things. . . .

For the time being do not be troubled by your desire to learn

more about our teaching about the origin of all things in a sim-
ple, uncreated, incorruptible good. There is time enough for
that. . . . Later, God willing, you will learn this and much more
about the origin and creation of all things when you have been
tested and found worthy to receive the apostolic tradition to
which we ourselves have succeeded. At that time we will prove all
these truths to you from the teaching of the Savior.

This has been a brief letter, my sister Flora. I have not tired
myself out, but have treated [these matters] cursorily and with
sufficient detail for an introduction. You will learn more in the
future, if you have become the fertile ground upon which the seed
has been thrown.

—FROM THE LETTER OF PTOLEMY TO FLORA PRESERVED IN
EPIPHANIUS'S *MEDICINE CHEST AGAINST ALL HERESIES* XXXIII.1–7

Ptolemy makes hierarchical distinctions in the purity and quality of biblical revelation as reflected in the three sources of the
law: there is the law that comes from God alone, the law that
Moses created, and the law that the elders promoted. At each
successive level the purity or sanctity diminishes, from the
purest and holiest to the most common and base.

A similar hierarchy of value and sanctity found expression in
Gnostic anthropology, the way Gnostics understood human
beings. For Gnostics three classes of people existed: the *hylic*
(from the Greek word *hyle,* meaning "matter"), the *psychic*
(from the Greek word *psyche,* meaning "soul"), and the *pneu-*
matic (from the Greek word *pneuma,* which means "spirit" or
"mind"). The same progression from materiality to spirituality
in the organization of the cosmos was replicated in the understanding of the three natures of human beings.

The hylic person was completely oriented toward the material world. The hylic person had no intimations of the divine spark, could not hear the call of the Savior, and was completely lacking in the insight or knowledge to begin an ascent toward the divine. The hylic was asleep and unaware, completely entrapped in the material world. Hylics existed as animated corpses, or as brute beasts, unable to understand either themselves or others, and they certainly could not comprehend the nature of God.

The psychic person was one step beyond the hylic. The psychic person had an inkling that the spiritual and divine realm existed. Psychic people knew enough to understand that the material world debilitated them, but not enough to perceive the divine spark, or to hear the call of the Savior, or to begin to ascend. Gnostic Christians considered regular churchgoing Christians to be psychic Christians. The psychic Christians at least knew that there is more to life than mere appearance and materiality, but they did not know how to transcend them.

The Gnostic was a pneumatic person. These people understood their election to ascent; they recognized the interior divine spark. They had heard the Savior's call, and they oriented themselves completely to their ascent to the divine realm. The pneumatics alone understood the true nature of the world as a demiurgic imitation of the true spiritual world of God. They alone pursued the knowledge necessary to progress through the cosmos toward divine union. Gnostics were by nature pneumatics; all other people must be either psychics or hylics.

The three categories revealed the fundamental nature of each person. The system explained why some people (the hylics) simply do not understand why others (the psychics) seem to understand and yet reject true knowledge, and why still others (the pneumatics) seem to thrive in the divine realm and eagerly pursue their exit from the material world and their entrance into the divine. From the Gnostic perspective, some people will never understand, others will catch a glimpse, and still others will come to true life and regeneration. The system explained not only the Gnostic identity, but also the relationship of the Gnostics to all the other people in their society.

The pneumatic person, the Gnostic, was engaged in the cosmic struggle for release from the imprisonment of the material world. This meant that the Gnostic experienced the self as alienated from the world; he or she actively resisted the effects of material existence. This struggle between the material and the divine did not arise because of a cosmic struggle between two equal forces, good and evil. The struggle arose rather in the desire to know the real, as opposed to the ephemeral and imaginary world, and to know the spiritual, as opposed to the false image of the real as it was poorly reflected in the demiurge's creation. The Gnostic's true home was the divine realm, the *pleroma*, not this alienating and confining world of materiality. One of the manuscripts found at Nag Hammadi was a partial translation of Plato's *Republic*—though Plato was no Gnostic, the Gnostics saw the world in some ways as Plato described it in his parable of the cave: as a shadowy simulacrum of a transcendent reality.

Gnostics experienced their pneumatic status while still locked in their bodies. The body served as the medium for their ascent until they could leave it behind altogether when they ascended beyond the final sphere. Gnostics used a number of different metaphors to express this transfigured bodily state. For example, Gnostic Christians compared their embodied lives to a body resurrected from the dead, a corpse that was filled with the divine presence, a bodily life already manifesting outwardly its inward divine spark. Gnostics spoke of themselves as already immortal. They understood their election as a guarantee of their eventual union with the divine and therefore they understood themselves, even in their embodied state, as having already achieved immortality. Hylics and psychics could not achieve this status: their nature condemned them to the confines of mortality. But the Gnostics could experience the wonder of their own regeneration and divinization while still in their bodies.

Gnostics looked in the world around them for signs of the regeneration they sought. They "read" other people and the cosmos in the same way they read their scriptures: they attempted to make sense of contradictions not by explaining them away, but by assigning them to different categories. That explained why the law of God came either from God, or Moses, or the elders of Israel. It also explained why some people never understand, others understand a little, and still others achieve an understanding that propels them toward ascent and union with God.

GNOSTIC SYSTEMS OF SALVATION

Soteriology is the study of systems of salvation. The Gnostics developed a very specific model of how salvation worked. Their system began with the Savior whom the supreme God sent to wake up the world. This Savior, as we will see in later chapters, was called by different names: Jesus, Christ, Messias, and Seth, just to name the most prominent ones.

In the Sophia myth, for example, the Savior descended into the material world to remind those capable of hearing that they have a divine spark within them. Unlike all other people who take on material existence, this Savior always remained fully awake. The Savior was a model for imitation by the Gnostics, as well as their guide back to the place of their origin. Salvation began with the response to the Savior's call and continued with the process of shedding the material body, ascending through the celestial spheres, and uniting with the supreme and truly spiritual God. The Gnostic's return restored what had been missing from the *pleroma* as a result of Sophia's arrogance and the false material creation of the demiurge; salvation completed the cycle.

GNOSTIC BIBLICAL INTERPRETATION

Biblical interpretation or exegesis was a primary tool that the Gnostics utilized in their return to the divine fullness. Ptolemy's letter is just one example. The scriptures provided the Gnostics with primary information, but they needed to understand the scriptures on a deeper level as well. The Gnostics' subtle interpretations of scriptures trained their minds so that they could see God properly.

The prologue and Saying 1 of the *Gospel of Thomas* shows

how Gnostics approached the sayings of Jesus: "These are the mysterious words of the living Jesus, which Jesus spoke and which Judas Thomas recorded. Anyone who finds the meaning of these words will live forever." In other words, interpretation can confer immortality!

Gnostic interpretations of the creation story in Genesis 1–2 led the Gnostics from a proper understanding of creation to their return to the paradise from which God expelled the original humans. The Gnostic system of salvation was concerned with much more than the fates of individual souls. In repairing what Sophia had broken, the Gnostics restored the divine fullness to God and to other divine beings. In this sense, the fate of the entire cosmos depended on their efforts.

DEMONS AND ANGELS

Gnostics believed that demons and angels ruled and controlled the body. Through various means, often associated with magic in the modern world, a Gnostic worked to wrest the body from its controlling forces. Knowing the names of the demons or angels that regulated a particular part of the body gave the Gnostic power over them. The *Apocryphon of John*, for example, describes the formation of Adam's body and gives the names of the demons associated with each part. The Gnostics could also enlist the support of good demons or angels to support them in their effort to control or transform their bodies and to counter the debilitating effects of materiality.

PRAYER AND MYSTICAL LANGUAGE

The Gnostic entered the divine fullness through prayer. The mind extending outward in prayer entered the divine fullness to join the *Aeons* (sacred beings that emanated from God—the word literally means "age" or "lifetime" in Greek) and other divine beings in their praise of the supreme and true God. In prayer, the Gnostic's mind literally left his or her body and entered the *pleroma,* a kind of foreshadowing of what would eventually happen to the Gnostic's whole being.

Often the Gnostic's prayer of praise erupted into a kind of mystical language, similar to the "speaking in tongues" or glossolalia experienced by charismatics throughout history. This language consisted of vowels set in various patterns that expressed the Gnostic's ecstatic experience. Like the parts of the body, the alphabet also had mystical power, especially the vowels. A passage from the *Allogenes* (61:3–17), a Nag Hammadi document, offers the following example:

> This is the son's thanksgiving for his enlightenment: "O Grace! After [I have experienced all] these things I thank you by singing you a hymn. For life has come down to me from you when you gave me wisdom. I praise you. I call you by that name hidden [deep] within me. a ô ee ô êêê ôôô ii ôôôô ooooo ôôôô uuuu ôô ôôôôôôôôô ôôôôôôô ôô ôô. You are [certainly] the one who lives in the spirit. Reverently, I sing you a hymn."

The Gnostics' mystical language used the power of these vowels in prayer as a means to propel them into an experience of the divine fullness and to project them further along the path of their own reunion with the divine realm.

THE SUCCESSION OF TEACHERS

Gnostic teachers passed on their secret knowledge and skill to their students, who in turn became teachers to still others. Ptolemy's letter to Flora mentioned an apostolic succession of teachers, from Jesus to the Christian apostles to the Gnostics themselves, and implied that, should Flora join his community, this knowledge would be passed on to her. The orthodox Christian churches appropriated the idea of apostolic succession from the Gnostics in order to counter their claim to special knowledge. In both the orthodox and the Gnostic camps, the phenomenon remained the same: their teachings were said to have been handed down to them directly from the Savior.

The Gnostics' sophisticated belief systems enrich our understanding of familiar Bible stories and parables. We'll close this chapter with the following selection from the Gnostic "Hymn of the Pearl" (from a Greek manuscript of the apocryphal *Acts of Thomas,* which I have slightly paraphrased), which traces their system of salvation in richly symbolic and poetic language—a splendid evocation of the richness and subtlety of Gnostic thought.

> When I was just a baby living in my Father's very wealthy and luxurious palace in the East, our native land, my parents provided me with great treasures from their enormous wealth and sent me off with it. . . . They took off

my bejeweled and gold-encrusted robe, which they had made for me because of their great love for me, and made a deal with me never to forget the robe with my name written on it. They said, "Travel to Egypt in search of the one pearl, which adorns the destructive serpent. If you return with it, we will return your gold-and-jewel-encrusted robe to you, and you will reign with us as the heir to our kingdom."

So off I went out of the East following a torturous and dangerous road. I had two guides because I was unfamiliar with the route. . . . As soon as we got to Egypt my two guides left me. So I went as fast as I could to find the serpent, whom I found asleep in his nest. I wanted to take the pearl from him.

So I changed my appearance to look like an alien, not like other Eastern people. I met another Easterner who looked like a regular free-born person, graceful and beautiful, a child of a noble family. This newfound friend came to live with me. I told him of my appointed task. I warned him about the Egyptians and their impurity. Then, in order to get the pearl from the snake, I put on Egyptian clothing so that I would not look like a stranger. I did not want the Egyptians waking the snake and pitting it against me.

By some strange means, though, the Egyptians figured out that I was a foreigner, and they sought to deceive me. I ate their food, and I forgot that I was a king's son, and I became a servant to the Egyptian king. I forgot all about the pearl. And because their food was so heavy, I fell into a deep sleep.

My parents became aware of this and grieved deeply. They sent out a proclamation to all the kingdom ... which everyone had to sign, saying: "From your Father the King of Kings and your mother who rules all the East, ... to our Son in Egypt: Remember the pearl that you were sent to retrieve from Egypt, and remember that you are royalty, for you have entered into bondage. Remember also your gold-encrusted robe. Your name is written in the Book of Life. ... " Then the king sealed the proclamation with his ring.

All of a sudden the proclamation flew down to me and became living speech. I took it and kissed it, eagerly read it. And I knew that it was conveying information that was written in my heart. Then I remembered the pearl I was sent to Egypt to reclaim. I began to weave magical charms against the wicked serpent. Using the powerful name of my Father, I put the serpent to sleep. Then I took the pearl from him and returned it to my parents. I took off the filthy clothes of the Egyptians and left their land in order to return home. As I traveled, I found the letter that awakened me. That letter had a voice and roused me when I slept, and it guided me as a light on the path homeward. All I could see before my eyes was the royal robe awaiting me.

THREE GNOSTIC SECTS

The writings of the early Christians who studied the so-called heresies (heresiologists) list many kinds of Gnostics. The foremost are the Sethians and Valentinians—everyone seemed concerned about their teachings. So I present them here. From among the varied Gnostics of lesser concern, I have chosen the Carpocratians, who had a very peculiar sort of Gnostic system, but one that provides a fascinating window on a kind of Gnostic practice.

WHO WERE THE SETHIANS?

For I am the first and the last.
I am the honored one and the scorned one.
I am the whore and the holy one.
I am the wife and the virgin.
I am the mother and the daughter.
I am the members of my mother.
I am the barren one and many are her sons.
I am she whose wedding is great, and I have not taken a husband.

—*THE THUNDER: PERFECT MIND* 13:16–25A, NHLE*

Nag Hammadi Library in English. NHLE citations refer to *The Nag Hammadi Library in English,* edited by James M. Robinson, HarperCollins, 1990 (revised edition). NHL refers to the *Nag Hammadi Library;* translations by the author.

The Sethians were like many people I know today who are spiritual seekers, who restlessly travel from one religion or spiritual tradition to another in search of wisdom. One of my friends is a typical example. She and I started out in the same Christian denomination, but she seemed to need more. Holding on to her Christianity, she began to do yoga. Then she added Hindu meditation. Next came New Age crystals and scents, then some Wiccan rituals. She seemed capable of expanding her horizons with each encounter. She never really gave up her Christianity; she simply added new traditions at each turn to expand her understanding and heighten her religious experience. This is how I understand the Sethian Gnostics. They were versatile and eager seekers who integrated every tradition they could find into their thought and practice.

Of all of the Gnostic sects, Sethian Gnosticism had the clearest sense of what constituted true knowledge. Like my friend, the Sethians moved from religion to religion, incorporating what seemed appropriate, forever combining and refining their knowledge. Their texts display the history of their pilgrimage through the intellectual world around them.

John D. Turner, in his essay "Sethian Gnosticism: A Literary History" (in *Nag Hammadi, Gnosticism, and Early Christianity,* edited by Charles Hedrick and Robert Hodgson, Hendrickson, 1986), describes the development of the Sethians from their origins in the first century B.C.E. as a baptismal sect that amalgamated Platonism with Jewish biblical interpretation. Then, in the first and early second centuries C.E., these Jewish Platonists adopted some Christian ideas and practices. By the third century Sethians had become dissatisfied with Christianity and moved away from it, splintering into a variety of Gnostic groups. Turner's history shows how the Sethians engaged with every movement that offered promise for developing the interior life and for perfecting its adherents. Much has been learned about Sethian teaching from the Nag Hammadi discovery, which yielded a rich lode of fifteen texts.

WHAT DID THE SETHIANS BELIEVE?

The Sethian Gnostics considered Seth, the third son of Adam in the book of Genesis, to be both a revealer and a savior. This is consistent: since knowledge saves, the revealer of mysterious knowledge is a vehicle of salvation. Here's a passage from the ending of the *Apocalypse of Adam*, an early and foundational Sethian text:

> Adam made these revelations known to Seth, his son.
> And the son taught his seed about them. This is Adam's
> concealed knowledge, given to Seth. It constitutes a holy
> baptism for those who understand the eternal knowledge
> that comes from those born of the word and the undestroyable illuminators. They came from the holy seed:
> Yesseus, Mazareus, Yassedekeus, the Living Water.

Adam gave knowledge to Seth, who in turn revealed that saving knowledge to those who had been baptized. This text displays all the familiar Gnostic elements: revelations, divine figures, baptismal rites, secret knowledge, a chosen and saved race of people. The playful reference to "Yesseus" (Jesus) suggested that this knowledge might even be good for Christians or come from Christians, and it was probably written during Sethian Gnosticism's period of engagement with Christianity, when Jesus would have been a representative of the savior Seth. Knowledge and salvation merge—a classic Gnostic system.

Sethians saw themselves as the direct descendants of Seth, the spiritual seed planted in the material world to provide for its redemption. The *Hypostasis of the Archons* ("The Reality of the Rulers"), another Sethian text from the Nag Hammadi archive, describes the Sethians' origins:

> You and your children come from the original father.
> Your souls come from above, from an indestructible light.
> Therefore the *archons* cannot approach them, because the spirit of truth dwells in them. And you who have their *gnosis* of this way live without death among dying people.

The seed of Seth bestowed immortality. The Sethians described themselves as an incorruptible race, a generation not ruled by a king, as the holy people of a great savior. The Sethians may have lived in the physical world marked by mortality, yet they also dwelt in a spiritual world where immortality reigned.

Sethian mythology was organized around a primary trinity: the Father (the Invisible Spirit), the Mother (*Barbelo*), and the Son (*Autogenes*, "the self-generated one," also sometimes called *Anthropos*, "the human one"). The *Apocryphon of John*, another Sethian text, amplified the three elements of the trinity: "[The Father] is the Invisible Spirit. Do not consider him a god or something like a god, because he is much more than a god. Nothing exists above him. No one rules over him. . . . He is completely perfect." It described the Mother as the Invisible

Spirit's first thought. The Invisible Spirit invested her with foreknowledge, indestructibility, eternal life, and truth. The Son, conceived by the Father and Mother, was pure light. The Sethians knew the Son as the Christ, the anointed one, who created the spiritual realm.

Sethians used the myth of Sophia to explain their concept of salvation. As recounted above, Sophia was one of the *Aeons* created by the Invisible Spirit, the Barbelo (Mother), and the Christ. Sophia desired to create something by herself without the consent of the Father. She willfully created what appeared to be a monstrous being, whom she called Yaltabaoth, but

---

Sethian Texts at Nag Hammadi

Allogenes

The Apocalypse of Adam

The Apocryphon of John

Eugnostos the Blessed

The Gospel of the Egyptians

The Hypostasis of the Archons

Hypsiphrone

Marsanes

Melchizedek

On the Origin of the World

The Thought of Norea

The Three Steles of Seth

The Thunder: Perfect Mind

The Trimorphic Protennoia

Zostrianos

---

whom others also called Saklas ("the fool") and Samael ("the blind"). Yaltabaoth, thinking himself to be the supreme Father, created the physical universe. Sophia repented of her willfulness, so the true Father attended to the seed of Seth by creating a path of salvation for Seth's descendants that would release them from the bondage of Yaltabaoth's physical universe. This path of salvation is hidden in the biblical narrative found in Genesis 2:4–3:24 and can only be discovered through deep exegesis. The outlines of the story may be familiar, but the theological significance that the Sethians derived from it is quite distant from traditional Jewish and Christian understanding.

Here is a Sethian interpretation of Paul's letters, which refers to the "blind" demiurge, who ignorantly and falsely thinks of himself as the one true God.

> *The great apostle [Paul], writing about the realities of the powers and inspired by the spirit of the Father of Truth, referred to the "powers of darkness" [Colossians 1:13] by saying "our fight is not against blood and flesh, but against the* archons *[i.e., rulers] of the universe and wicked spirits" [Ephesians 6:12]. So I send you this treatise because you inquire about the reality of the rulers. [First of all,] their chief ruler is blind, because he said powerfully, ignorantly, and arrogantly, "I am God, and there is no other God than me." Saying this he sinned against the* pleroma. *His speech rose up to the incorruptible realm, and a voice from that incorruptible realm burst forth announcing, "You are wrong, Samael," which means "god of the blind."*
>
> —FROM *HYPOSTASIS OF THE ARCHONS* ("REALITIES OF THE RULERS"), NHL

The Sethians believed they were the central characters in a great saga of the salvation of themselves and their world. They experienced themselves as living both in and out of time: in time for the appearance of Seth, and out of time to escape from the bonds of mortality. They divided history into three periods, each with its own savior: Noah's great flood, the fire of Sodom and Gomorrah, and the Judgment. Seth appeared during each of those periods to save his seed. The story of Adam and Eve was a prologue; the rescue of the spiritual seed of Seth in the Roman period was the culminating event.

The *Apocalypse of Adam* recounts in sublime language the history of the succession of thirteen kingdoms and their leaders. The description of each of these kingdoms ends with the phrase, regarding the leader, "And thus he came to the water." This connection of historical periods with baptism culminated in the establishment of the final people, "the generation without a King over it," the Sethian Gnostics, who no longer submit to any authority save that of the supreme Father. In fact, Sethians saw their personal and collective salvation as intimately connected—not only with the salvation of the cosmos, but with the salvation of every people in every age.

In the surviving religious treatises, the mysterious language of "descent" and "ascent" appears often, correlating the knowledge of the savior's descent to the experience of the Gnostics' ascent. The Nag Hammadi text *Allogenes* describes how Gnostics were trained to move up the path of ascent. Knowledge and experience fused in the ballet of descending and ascending.

The Sethians also articulated a kind of negative theology, which may be difficult to grasp at first. In the Western religious tradition, most mystics practice negative theology, which seeks to experience God by first ascribing a category to the divinity

("God is good") and then negating it ("but God far surpasses every known good"), in order to bring a person to knowledge in unknowing. The *Apocryphon of John* described the Father, the Invisible Spirit, in this way:

> He is a pure, holy, spotless and inestimable light. He is unutterable, since he is perfect in incorruptibility. He is not [known] in perfection, nor in beatitude, nor in deity, but he is far superior [to all these categories]. He is not embodied nor is he bodiless. He is neither large nor is he small. No means exists to answer, "What is his quantity?" or "What is his quality?" for no one can know him. He does not exist as one person among others, rather he exists far superior [to them], but his substance does not participate in the *aeons* nor in time.

Negative theology expressed the sublime nature of God while acknowledging the utter inability of humans to comprehend a divinity that so surpassed any human categories of knowledge. Sethians readily acknowledged their inability to know the Invisible Spirit and their simultaneous experience of his glory and presence both within them and outside them.

Sethian prayers and hymns expressed both the mystery of negative theology and the wonder of ascent. The *Three Steles of Seth* consists of seven hymns of praise, ending with the following instruction:

> Those who recall these [hymns] and perpetually praise will indeed become perfect among all other perfect beings. They will become supremely impassive. For to-

gether and alone they sing praises, and then they become silent. And just as they were ordered, they ascend. After they become silent, they descend from the third; then they sing praises to the second, and then the first. The way of ascent is the way of descent.

At each phase of ascent and descent, the Sethian Gnostic prayed and sang ecstatically. The *Gospel of the Egyptians* exemplifies that ecstasy in a prayer:

> I bear your great name, O *Autogenes,* the perfect one who resides within me. You who appear to everyone, I see you. . . . Knowing you now, I have blended myself with the immutable. I have put on the armor of light. In fact, I have become light. . . . I glorify you truly, for I have understood you, *sou ies ide aeio aeie ois,* O *aion, aeon,* O silent God. I honor you. I rest in you, O Son *es es o e,* the one without form who dwells in those without form.

These ecstatic and mystical prayers literally carried the mind upward to the divine realm to pray and to praise, to be silent and to sing hymns, to rest and to begin to descend.

So much of the Sethian literature was destroyed—or deliberately distorted by the heresiologists' paraphrases—that we only rarely encounter it directly. But sometimes they appended personal notes to the ends of their treatises. The scribe of the *Gospel of the Egyptians* has even given us his name:

> The Gospel of the Egyptians. This book inscribed by God, holy and secret. Let grace, knowledge, perception,

and self-control attend the one who has written it, Eugnostos the beloved in the Spirit. In the flesh my name is
Gongessos, and I am one of the community of the incorruptible lights. The holy book of the great, Invisible
Spirit is inspired by God. Amen.

This scribe bore two names, one in the flesh, Gongessos, and
one in the Sethian community, Eugnostos, which means literally "well-knowing." He prayed for his own enlightenment
while also commending the book as sacred and inspired, and in
doing so he revealed the intensity and joy of these indefatiga-
ble believers as they communicated divine *gnosis* to one another
on their mystical path into the divine.

The Sethians were one of the most intriguing and compelling of the Gnostic communities. Many of their doctrines
and beliefs found their way into mainstream Christian teachings on prayer and the ascent to the divine, negative theology
and the Trinity, and the uses of Platonic thought in theology. Despite the orthodox church's untiring efforts to exclude
them, the Sethians had a dramatic and lasting impact on
Christianity.

WHO WERE THE VALENTINIAN GNOSTICS?

*Light and darkness, life and death, right and left, are brothers of one an-
other. They are inseparable. Because of this neither are the good good, nor
the evil evil, nor is life life, nor death death. For this reason each one will*

dissolve into its earliest origin. But those who are exalted above the world
are indissoluble, eternal.

—*THE GOSPEL OF PHILIP* 53:14B–23A, NHLE

If the Sethian Gnostics were like New Age seekers, tirelessly exploring other religious traditions for whatever divine wisdom they could glean from them, the Valentinians were like professors of theology—learned, self-confident, not a little conceited. Though Christian, the Valentinians made no bones about the low regard in which they held the vast majority of their co-religionists, whom they considered to be little more than imbeciles. Only Valentinian knowledge could make sense of the scriptures and explain how their revelations cohered; only the Valentinians could show the way toward union with God. Or at least so they thought. The Valentinians never left the church; rather, the church kicked them out.

Here is Irenaeus on the Valentinian *Gospel of Truth* (*Against Heresies,* III.11.9). He can hardly contain his disgust at their presumption.

> But Valentinus's people are completely frivolous because they write their own books and pride themselves in having more gospels than really exist. Truly, they have such a high degree of audaciousness that they give the title to their very new writing, "The Gospel of Truth." But that gospel has nothing in common with the gospels of the apostles. It is not really a gospel; it is filled with blasphemy. If what they have published is the Gospel of Truth, so dissimilar from those given to us by the apostles, any-

one can see that what the apostles have given us cannot
be considered a gospel of truth. All you need to do is look
at the scriptures themselves [and compare them].

It is interesting to contrast the actual words of a Valentinian
treatise with Irenaeus's bilious characterization of it. Many
scholars believe Valentinus himself was the author of the *Gospel
of Truth,* whose opening lines appear below. It is self-evidently
neither frivolous nor blasphemous; but it does perhaps imply
that some well-meaning Christians remain trapped in error,
fruitlessly searching creation for answers that can be found only
in the supernal realms.

The gospel of truth is [sheer] joy for the ones who have
obtained the grace of knowing him from the Father of
truth. [This grace came] by means of the Word's power,
which proceeded from the fullness. This [Word] exists in
the thinking and the mind of the Father. It is the one
called "the Savior," because that names his work, to redeem those who do not know the Father. The [Word's]
proclamation is a gospel of hope, a discovery for those
searching for him.

The totality searched about for the one from whom all
things had issued. [But the totality did not understand]
that the totality already existed within the one [whom
they sought]. [The one whom they sought] is the incomprehensible and inconceivable one who is superior to
every manner of thinking. [This futile search for something already within] created ignorance of the Father, and
that ignorance created torment and panic. That torment

grew like a fog so that no one could see any longer. That explains why error became so powerful. Not knowing the truth, it foolishly explored its own matter. It explored the creation, powerfully and beautifully preparing the substitute for the truth.

Perhaps of all the adherents to Gnostic systems, Valentinian Gnostics posed the greatest threat to orthodox Christianity. They supported the church as a recruiting ground for potential members, while at the same time calling into question its theological and intellectual stature. They were the first to write commentaries on the scriptures (especially the Epistles of Paul and the Gospel of John) to elucidate their deeper meanings for their followers. The orthodox churches would follow suit, providing exegeses of their own, and the wars of scriptural interpretation would never end, continuing even to our own day. The Valentinian Gnostics set the basic parameters for the development of Christian theology, even though they lost the battle for teaching their version of it within the churches.

The Valentinian school was founded by the philosopher Valentinus (ca. 100–175 C.E.). He was educated in Alexandria, Egypt, the primary center for philosophical, scientific, religious, and literary study in the ancient world. Sometime around 136 Valentinus came to Rome, where he participated actively in the churches and became a very successful Christian teacher and a revered expositor of the deep meaning of scripture. He moved to Cyprus in 160, after he lost an election for bishop of Rome. That he could have even been seen as worthy to be considered for an episcopate shows the great regard in which his teachings were held.

The Valentinian school attracted some superb students: Ptolemy, whose letter to Flora was excerpted above; Heracleion, known best for his brilliant and controversial commentary on the Gospel of John; Theodotus, whose writings were collected by Clement of Alexandria; and Marcus, best known for his numerological and magical practices.

Valentinus and his followers all remained members of the local Christian church. They regarded regular church teachings, the catechesis, as appropriate for the ordinary, or psychic level of believer—and as a kind of preparatory education for the deeper spiritual teachings provided by the Gnostics. The Valentinian *Treatise on the Resurrection,* discovered at Nag Hammadi, describes the difference between simple and profound levels of study:

> My son Rheginos, many people want to study many things when they have a question for which they need an answer. If they succeed in finding their answer they usually consider themselves great. But, I think, they have not really studied from within the Word of Truth. In fact, they simply seek their own rest—the rest that we have received comes from our Savior, the Lord Christ. We received the rest when we acquired knowledge of the truth and rested ourselves solidly upon it.

The Valentinians considered those who have found an answer and stopped there to be far inferior to those who have sought a deep knowledge and found true rest in their seeking. The inferior person belonged only to the psychic church, while the superior seeker belonged to the pneumatic.

WHAT DID THE VALENTINIANS BELIEVE?

Most Valentinian teaching revolved about the reading of scripture and the elucidation of the rites of the church. The Valentinians parsed and reparsed the scriptures, digging past the literal events of Jesus' life, his crucifixion, and his resurrection to uncover the mysterious information necessary for the Gnostic to find true salvation. For example, the *Treatise on the Resurrection* explains the significance of the resurrection:

> You are not ignorant of the fact that the Savior swallowed up death, because he overcame the perishable world. Transforming himself into an imperishable *Aeon,* he raised himself up. The invisible swallowed up the visible, and the Savior provided us with a way of salvation. This is exactly as the apostle said, "We suffered with him, and we were resurrected with him, and we ascended to heaven with him." Now if we show ourselves in this world as wearing him, we become his beams, and he embraces us until our own setting, our own death. He drives us to heaven, like the beams of the sun, unrestrained in any way. This truly is a spiritual resurrection that swallows up the psychic just as he swallowed up the fleshly.

Even Irenaeus, who was the first to attack Valentinian teachings, admitted in his treatise *Against Heresies* (I.3.6) that such readings were both intelligent and subtle.

Valentinian teaching is not easy to summarize. Its cosmology is very complex but worth describing in broad terms. In the Valentinian system, the cosmos was created through a series of emanations from an original pair or dyad (the Ineffable and Si-

Major Valentinian Texts at Nag Hammadi

The Gospel of Truth

The Gospel of Philip

The Treatise on the Resurrection

The Exegesis on the Soul

A Valentinian Exposition

lence), which in turn created by their union another dyad (Parent and Truth), which in turn created four other spiritual beings (the World, Life, Human Being, Church), all of which made up the *pleroma,* the divine Fullness. These spiritual beings in turn created thirty *Aeons,* subordinate spiritual entities, who joined the superior spiritual entities to sing hymns of praise to the Fullness. It is noteworthy that the names of each of the spiritual figures above had philosophical significance (such as Silence, Truth, Church). Giving a name to something ineffable renders it substantial, or hypostatizes it. In their creation story, the Valentinians connected the generation of philosophical concepts to the creation of the spiritual realm, and then, as we will see below, related the physical world back to that conceptual framework.

One of the *Aeons,* the Mother, fell from grace and from that fall originated the created physical universe. Irenaeus (*Against Heresies* I.11.1) explained it this way: the Mother revolted and crossed the boundary that separated her from the Fullness and from the Parent. Remembering the divine realm, however, the Mother produced two figures: the Savior and the Shadow. The

Savior, however, separated from the Shadow and returned to the Fullness. The Mother, now remaining with only the Shadow, produced the Demiurge as the supreme God of everything he created. Jesus was the Savior who separated from the Mother and ascended to the Fullness. Truth produced the Holy Spirit as a guide through the *Aeons*. The Savior, who was Jesus, was sent again from the Fullness to the created world in order to restore lost people to spiritual salvation by undoing the debilitating effects of material existence caused by the Mother's fall.

In the Valentinian view, the goal of human endeavor was to trace the way through the merely physical and psychical existence created by the Demiurge back to the contemplation of the divine sphere, the Fullness. Valentinians guided others through the salvation process by imitating the work of the Savior.

This system explained not only how the physical universe was generated but also the vast extent of the spiritual universe available to those capable of contemplating it and entering it through meditation and prayer. And Valentinians tried to do this within the framework of the Christian scriptures and liturgical traditions. Irenaeus explains their approach in this way:

> They [the Valentinians] tell us that this knowledge has not been openly disclosed because not everyone has the ability to receive it. Rather [they argue] that the Savior mystically revealed the knowledge in the parables to those proven capable of understanding it. This is how they do it. The thirty Aeons refers to the thirty years during which the Savior did nothing in public, and to the laborers in the vineyard [that is, those sent out at the third, sixth, and ninth hours]. They also argue that Paul often directly refers to the Aeons when he

writes, "To all the generations of the aeons *of the* aeon.*" Yes, they ar-*
gue that we refer to the Aeons *even when we conclude our Eu-*
charist with the words "To aeons *of* aeons*" [forever and ever].*

—*AGAINST HERESIES* 1.3.1

Here we see how Valentinians ascribed deeper meanings to basic formulas of Christian worship, such as the traditional ending of prayers with the phrase "forever and ever" (literally "to
aeons of *aeons*" in Greek, which they interpreted as referring
to the *Aeons,* beings of the spiritual realm). Unexplained and
seemingly trivial details and numbers in the scriptures (such as
Jesus' thirty years of earthly life, the hours at which the labor-
ers in the vineyards were sent out, and the multiplication of the
grain that produced thirty- and sixty-fold) all became opportu-
nities for the Valentinians to reveal profound philosophical, religious, and mystical meanings that would have remained
hidden from ordinary psychic Christians.

The Valentinians taught that the existing sacraments of the
church also had deeper meaning—and they created new sacraments of their own as well. Sacraments are ritual acts that
embody and make manifest in physical life the realities and
graces of the spiritual realm. The orthodox sacraments of the
time most likely included baptism, the Eucharist, chrism (the
anointing of the sick with oil), and ordination (the laying on of
hands for commissioning missionaries and apostles). Valentinian sacraments, or "mysteries," as described in the Nag Hammadi *Gospel of Philip,* included these and also the mystery of
Redemption and the Bridal Chamber: "The Lord did everything in a mystery, a baptism and a chrism and a eucharist and
a redemption and a bridal chamber."

Valentinians imbued the sacraments of the orthodox church with Gnostic meaning: baptism conferred resurrection and immortality and remade the person, much as dye changes the color of cloth. Chrism bestowed the divine light, enabling the Gnostic to see the spiritual world. The *Gospel of Philip* quotes part of the fulfillment prayer: "He said on that day in the thanksgiving, 'You who have joined the perfect light with the Holy Spirit, unite the angels with us also, as being the images.' " The Valentinians also developed their own sacraments. The Redemption celebrated the permanent release of the Gnostic from the bonds of the demiurge, a release effected both ritually and through *gnosis*. And the Bridal Chamber celebrated the complete union of the Gnostic with the divine realm, a permanent and immutable status of perfection and rest, which characterizes the goal of Valentinian Gnostic life. A Valentinian inscription found at the Via Latina in Rome and housed at the Capitoline Museum shows the relationship of some of the Valentinian sacraments. It is a four-line poem, here translated in prose:

> Carry a torch for me for bathing [in water], my fellow brothers of the bridal chamber. [It is for] banquets in our rooms that they hunger, extolling the Father and praising the Son. In that place may there be a single well and a flowing [spring] of truth.

The Valentinian system made sense of things that otherwise seemed incomprehensible; this probably explains why it was so popular, despite its elite mentality and intellectual complexity. Had Valentinus been elected bishop of Rome, the very face of Christianity would be different today. Certainly the worship and the scriptures would remain the same, as well as the ethics and concern for the poor, but the intellectual life of the church would have been far more developed, more intense, more vigorous, and less timid in its theological explorations. The Christian church of Rome might have supplanted Alexandria as the intellectual center for early Christianity.

WHO WERE THE CARPOCRATIANS?

For I am knowledge and ignorance.
I am shame and boldness.
I am shameless; I am ashamed.
I am strength and I am fear.
I am war and peace.
Give heed to me.
I am the one who is disgraced and the great one.

—*THE THUNDER: PERFECT MIND* 14:26–35A, NHLE

Earlier in this book, I said that Gnostics were accused of everything from incest to cannibalism. The Carpocratians, a Gnostic sect founded by Carpocrates of Alexandria in the first half of the second century C.E., were widely condemned for their depravity during the four centuries of their existence; they and their "unspeakable teachings" figure prominently in a controversy that has roiled the world of Bible studies for the past forty years.

It began in 1958 when Morton Smith, a professor at Columbia University, was cataloging texts in the library of Mar

Saba, a 1,500-year-old monastery that is carved into the walls of a desert canyon near Bethlehem. Smith glanced at the end-papers of a printed book dating from the seventeenth century and discovered a handwritten copy of a letter from Clement of Alexandria, the great second-century Christian teacher, that was addressed to an otherwise unknown individual named Theodore, who had apparently been involved in disputes with the Carpocratians. Not only has its original never been found, no other copy of this letter (actually a fragment of a letter—it is tantalizingly incomplete) exists. Smith photographed the letter and returned the book to the shelf; eventually he would publish several books and articles about it. (See Appendix 1 for the complete text of the letter.)

Clement's letter responded to questions that Theodore had asked him about an edition of the Gospel of Mark that he had seen which contained episodes that were unfamiliar to him, including one where Jesus raised a wealthy young man from the dead and then instructed him in the mysteries of the Kingdom of God. The narrative seems to fit neatly between the canonical Mark's 10:34 (Jesus' prediction of his persecution, death, and resurrection) and 10:35 (James's and John's request for special status). Clement recognized the passage; he knew precisely what Theodore had read. It was a rank forgery, the unmistakable handiwork of the notorious Carpocratians.

WHAT DID THE CARPOCRATIANS BELIEVE?

Epiphanius wrote that Carpocrates "taught his followers to perform every obscenity and every sinful act." Carpocratians

believed that the physical world was the base creation of inferior angels; God had never taken any personal interest in this
world or its inhabitants. Then Jesus, a normal, flesh-and-blood
man whose father was Joseph, was baptized and his immortal
soul awakened. Suddenly he "perfectly remembered those
things that he had witnessed within the sphere of the unbegotten God." After his awakening, Jesus was able to resist the in-
vidious effects of his materiality and ascend to the supreme
God; thus empowered, he taught others how to make the ascent as well.

It was here that Carpocratian theology of salvation took a
strange turn. Since the world was illusory and godless, the Carpocratians declared that good and evil could not have any objective existence; they were merely categories that had been
invented by the minds of men. Carpocratians also believed in
reincarnation, or as Irenaeus put it, "the transmigration [of the
soul] from body to body." These seemingly separate beliefs—
that the world is utterly godless, that good and evil are subjec-
tive categories, and that souls travel from body to body—all
came together in the Carpocratian model of salvation.

Before material creation could be transcended, the Carpocratians believed, it had to be experienced thoroughly. Irenaeus explained: "souls should have experience of every kind of
life as well as every kind of action" so that they might be released from the physical world and ascend like Jesus to the
spiritual realm. "In this way," Irenaeus continued, "all souls are
saved, whether their own, which, guarding against all delay,
participate in all sorts of actions during one incarnation, or
those, again, who, by passing from body to body, are set free, on
fulfilling and accomplishing what is requisite in every form of

life into which they are sent, so that at length they shall no longer be shut in the body."

The release from the bondage of the material world and the ascent of the soul to its original home imitated Jesus. Jesus was the un-incarnate one who led the way for the incarnate ones to escape the cycle of reincarnation and return to the unbegotten—but the path to the spiritual led first through every experience of the world—including even the most base and corrupt. Just how corrupt is not clear; but several church authorities attested to the fact that the Carpocratians held their wives in common and didn't respect private property. It was perhaps Christianity's first encounter with antinomianism, Martin Luther's term for the belief that if good works didn't lead the way to salvation then neither did evil works hinder it.

Now back to Clement and Theodore. Clement began his letter with a sound condemnation of the Carpocratians for their carnality: "bragging that they are free, they have become subject to their base lusts." He contested the Carpocratian concept that categories of good and evil are human creations with the argument that faith declares some things good and other things evil: "Such men are to be opposed in all ways and altogether. For, even if they should say something true, one who loves the truth should not, even so, agree with them. For not all true things are the truth, nor should that truth which merely seems true according to human opinions be preferred to the true truth, that according to the faith."

Clement then went on to explain that the Carpocratians had altered the mystical edition of the Gospel of Mark to justify their evil practices. But it was more complicated than that. Even before the Carpocratians came along, there had been two different versions of the Gospel of Mark. The first, original version did not contain any esoteric teaching, but was intended for the general public. Clement described it this way: "Mark . . . narrated the Lord's activities, though he did not discuss all of his deeds nor did he suggest any secret things. Rather Mark chose what seemed the most helpful for increasing the faith of the people undergoing instruction." This is the gospel for the simple believer.

But after Peter's death, Mark traveled from Rome to Alexandria, where he "wrote a more spiritual gospel to be used by those people seeking perfection." This esoteric gospel for the spiritually perfect, the *Secret Gospel of Mark,* added other episodes—such as the story of the young man raised from the dead that Theodore had been so startled to read—and teachings not found in the gospel for simple believers. Mark "included certain sayings that he, precisely because he was a mystagogue, knew would lead seekers into the most exclusive temple of truth enshrouded by seven veils."

What is a "mystagogue"? A person who initiates others into mystical secrets. All religious traditions have them, not just Christian Gnosticism. In the orthodox Christian monasteries, for example, elder monks would act as mystagogues when they helped novices learn to live the monastic life. Clement calls Mark a mystagogue; in the *Secret Gospel of Mark,* Mark portrays Jesus as one as well. In fact, as we will soon see, it is precisely because Jesus was so characterized that there has been so much controversy about this letter. Precisely what did Jesus do when he initiated his followers into the mysteries?

And precisely what are the greater mysteries? The Greek term for a sacrament was *mysterion,* a mystery. The mysteries of baptism and the Eucharist were the basic sacraments of the early church. Baptism initiated a person into the Body of Christ; the Eucharist joined the person to the mystical presence of Christ made real in the bread and the wine. These were the lesser mysteries. The greater mysteries comprised mostly secret teachings handed over from mystagogues to their most advanced students.

Now back to the letter and the *Secret Gospel of Mark*. According to Clement, Carpocrates, instructed by demons and using "foul arts," enslaved a presbyter of the church in Alexandria and got him to hand over a copy of the esoteric *Secret Gospel of Mark*. Not only did Carpocrates interpret it according to his blasphemous and carnal doctrines, he "polluted" it by interpolating his own words into the manuscript, "mixing with the spotless and holy words utterly shameless lies." This, Clement declared, was the gospel that Theodore had seen.

Modern scholars had long suspected that more than one version of the Gospel of Mark had circulated in the ancient world. Clement's letter, painstakingly copied into a book some fifteen hundred years after it was written, and then fortuitously discovered almost three hundred years after that, confirmed their suspicion. One version of the gospels was intended for simple Christians (psychic Christians, as the Gnostics would say), the other for the spiritually advanced (pneumatic). But what depravities had the Carpocratians introduced into this hitherto unsuspected third version?

As we have seen, the *Secret Gospel of Mark* tells how Jesus was brought to the tomb of a rich young man by his sister. He raised him from the dead and instructed him. And "when it was evening, the young man went to him with a linen cloth draped over his naked body." The two men passed the night together, while Jesus taught him the mystery of the Kingdom of God.

All of that material is true, Clement told Theodore, but by no means should he believe the part about "naked man with naked man"—that is one of the Carpocratian alterations. And after just a few more lines (frustratingly, right after Clement promises "the true explanation even according to the true philosophy"), the fragment comes to an end.

Wait a minute: *"Naked man with naked man"*? Now perhaps you understand why Theodore was so nonplussed by what he'd read. Needless to say, that phrase set off a firestorm when Morton Smith presented his discovery to the scholarly world. Modern-day heresiologists castigated Smith and called his integrity into question, contemporary analogues of the Carpocratians—an obscure religious sect in California that practices free love and advocates gay liberation—drew him into their figurative embrace, and any number of latter-day Clements attempted to explain the controversy away.

Did an ancient version of the Gospel of Mark that declared that Jesus and the boy were naked together really exist? Was the *Secret Gospel of Mark*'s big secret that Jesus was a practicing homosexual? Could Smith be a hoaxer? Surprisingly, considering how little physical evidence exists to support Smith's discovery, the philological and linguistic evidence is strong. The scholarly consensus is that Clement's letter to Theodore is indeed authentic.

Were the Carpocratians so shameless that they libeled Jesus—or were the heresiologists so eager to protect Jesus' reputation for chastity that they libeled the Carpocratians? Could

Jesus, acting as a mystagogue, have employed tantric-like practices when he initiated the youth into the mysteries, to create an ecstatic experience? Was the language simply metaphorical? The battle continues.

The *Secret Gospel of Mark* opens an amazing window into the varieties of early Christianity as they vied with each other, not only to produce a "true" gospel, but about the most basic tenets of faith and morality.

4

A NON-GNOSTIC CHALLENGE TO ORTHODOXY

Some also heard from Polycarp [a revered bishop who was martyred] that the Lord's disciple John, entering a bathhouse in Ephesus, saw Cerinthus [a known heretic] there. John ran out of the baths screaming, "Get out of here. The bathhouse itself might collapse because Cerinthus, truth's enemy, is inside." And Polycarp himself responded to Marcion, who when meeting him asked, "Do you know me?" Polycarp answered, "I do indeed know you, firstborn of Satan."

—IRENAEUS, *AGAINST HERESIES* III.4

Among the early Christians were sects that radically challenged some of the core beliefs of the orthodox church. These groups—like some fundamentalist Christians today—had a few nonnegotiable bedrock beliefs that they used as a litmus test to settle every question, from which books of the Bible were legitimate to how Christians should live their lives. This principle-based intellectualism differs from the Gnostics' approach to theology. Gnostics made an effort to blend their own intellectual tradition with that of the psychic churches, supplementing, but not supplanting, their theological and biblical teachings.

The principle-based believers, on the other hand, were revisionists and reformers. They came to certain conclusions and then tried to mold the church and its scriptures to suit their beliefs. They edited known gospels, developed new gospels, or even founded independent churches based exclusively on their own principles. These alternative churches often retained all the trappings of the orthodox church—ordained leaders, teachers, organization, mission, liturgies, and sacraments—but their teachings were quite different. The challenges they presented and the reactions they precipitated would have a long-lasting effect on the orthodox church. Such were the Marcionites.

WHO WERE THE MARCIONITES?

Like some of today's television-star evangelists, there were ancient preachers who became wealthy enough to buy or to build their own churches. Marcion of Sinope (ca. 85–160 C.E.), a prosperous shipowner from the seaport of Pontus on the Black Sea (modern Turkey), was one of them. When he moved from Pontus to Rome (probably to engage in the lucrative Roman shipping business), he presented the Roman church with a gift of 200,000 sesterces, a huge fortune, comparable to the price of entry into the Roman nobility, and tried to use the influence it bought to permanently alter the church. According to Tertullian (*Against Marcion* 1:19), in July of 144 C.E. the Roman church condemned his teachings, excommunicated him, and returned his gift. He reinvested it in a church of his own, purified and reformed based on his principles. These Marcionite churches spread throughout the Roman Empire, especially in the eastern empire and beyond. Evidence exists for their survival well into the fifth century C.E.

THE MARCIONITE SCRIPTURES

So what was Marcion's problem with orthodox Christianity? What was the basis of his dissent and reform? When Marcion read the scriptures of the Old and New Testaments, he could not understand how the God of the Old Testament and the God of Jesus in the New Testament could be one and the same. For Marcion, the God of the Israelites appeared to be vengeful, judgmental, and angry, constantly sending prophets to upbraid his people for failing to meet his standards, and inflicting floods and other catastrophes on them when his patience gave out. To Marcion, this God seemed both unfaithful and contradictory in nature. In comparison, the God of the New Testament was loving and consistent, oriented toward peace and brotherly love, and eager to heal people, both physically and spiritually. One God was oriented toward law and retribution, the other toward love and mercy.

Marcion concluded that they were in fact two entirely different Gods. The creator God of the Old Testament was a lesser demiurgic God; his whimsical, violent, and irrational creation stood in opposition to the true God, the God of Jesus, whose world was loving and consistent. The demiurge had total sway over the physical world, while the God of Jesus controlled the spiritual world. The twain would never meet.

The Gnostic myths may have allowed that the world was created by a lesser divinity, but they never denied that the true spiritual God played a role in the Hebrew Bible. They resolved the conundrum of God's personality by reading allegorically. The literal text was simply a jumping-off point for further study; the real import of scripture was not necessarily to be found on its surface. For both Gnostics and orthodox Christians, exegesis was enough to smooth over the rough edges between the Old Testament and the New. Properly interpreted, the two parts of the Bible told a larger story of salvation—a steady and consistent progression leading from the Creation to the Second Coming of Christ.

Marcion, however, rejected allegorical and spiritual readings of the scriptures as unfaithful to truth—to use the modern technical term, he was a literalist, a literal reader of the Bible. Read literally, and without the benefit of any glosses, he found so much of the Bible to be so objectionable that he decided it couldn't possibly be God's Word. So first he rejected the Old Testament in its entirety. Then he set about purging the New Testament of its many allusions to the Old Testament, which he presumed had been incorporated by biased editors. He became the first textual critic of the New Testament, only instead of using philological and historical criteria to identify the sources of its texts, he edited and shaped it to fit his theological principles.

And Marcion was as fearless a critic as he was rigorous. He determined that the gospels of Matthew, Mark, and John were so corrupt that he threw them out in their entirety. Only Luke's gospel could be trusted, because it presents Jesus in a much more Roman than Jewish way, as a kind of holy man who only passes through the physical world on his way to the spiritual, resurrected world. Yet even Luke's gospel needed to be radically altered.

Marcion did not believe that Jesus had a human body. If Jesus never became incarnate, then he could not have been born of a human mother. So in addition to the Old Testament allusions, all the birth narratives, including Luke's, needed to be deleted. Presumably, although it is difficult to say for sure since only fragments of the Marcionite Bible have come down to us, Marcion also adjusted the crucifixion in order to deemphasize the physical killing of Jesus on the cross. And he passed over the resurrection without comment because if Jesus didn't die then his resurrection would be superfluous.

Marcion's Bible retained ten of Paul's letters, again "cleansed" of problematically Jewish material, so that Paul's pure message of grace and salvation could shine through. He "corrected" the texts of Galatians, 1 and 2 Corinthians, Romans, 1 and 2 Thessalonians, Ephesians (which Marcion knew as Laodiceans), Colossians, Philemon, and Philippians, and gathered them into a book he called *Apostolikon*. Those texts, plus the revised Gospel of Luke (the *Euagellion*), were the Marcionite Bible.

A comparison of Marcion's and the canonical Philippians 2:6 and 7 is revealing. Marcion omitted only a few words but he changed the text's meaning completely, so that Jesus never really takes on human flesh, but has only the appearance of human embodiment:

Who, existing in the form of God, he did not consider being equal to God something to be grasped, but emptying himself, he took on the form of a slave, [and] he came to exist in a human likeness and was found in the form of a human.

—PHILIPPIANS 2:6–7

Marcion's version is this:

Who, existing in the form of God, he did not consider being equal to God something to be grasped, but emptying himself, he took on the form of a slave in a human likeness, being found in the form of a human.

(See Appendix 2 for more information on Marcion's New Testament canon.)

MARCIONITE THEOLOGY

Marcion described Jesus' body as a mere phantasm, a physical illusion, or an ephemeral appearance. If Jesus did not have a body, and if Christians must imitate the life of Jesus, then it stands to reason that a believer should reject the physical body, too. The Marcionites did not shy from this conclusion. They were celibate; they rejected the personal use of money and embraced a life of poverty. The Marcionites became ascetics precisely to imitate Jesus and to obey his injunctions not to worry about food or clothing.

The problem with Jesus' physical body emerges from the problem of the demiurge. If the demiurge—a false and lowly god—created the physical world, then Jesus could not possibly have entered into it enfleshed. And if Jesus did not have a real body, then real Christians ought to strive to cast off their own, to create a heavenly body on earth that would undo the effects of the demiurge.

Although he held some beliefs in common with the Gnostics, particularly with regard to the demiurgic creation, Marcion was not a Gnostic. Unlike the Gnostics, Marcion did not create complex philosophical or theological systems; nor did he engage in the kind of expansive thinking empowered by allegorical and spiritual interpretation of the scriptures. His rejection of the Old Testament resulted in an impoverished understanding of history and historical development; unlike the Gnostics and the orthodox church, he did not acknowledge an overarching biblical narrative that reveals God working through history, steadily guiding humanity toward salvation. Marcion didn't believe that Jesus came to save the world, either—to him it was hopelessly unredeemable. Salvation was possible only to the extent that people rejected the world. If the Gnostics sought to enhance church teaching, Marcion sought to purify and radically simplify it.

Marcion's church retained the orthodox structure, with himself as bishop. The church order consisted of bishops, presbyters (priests), and deacons. They celebrated the same liturgies, although probably significantly altered to accommodate Marcionite theology.

Marcion's profession as a shipping magnate gave him access to the widest possible geographic venue for spreading his church. His embrace of poverty in the midst of a very lucrative business assured him the financial resources to build a church that would give the orthodox churches a run for their money. And it did.

The appeal of the Marcionite churches and the key to their

longevity probably resided in the fact that there were no contradictions to be explained away; Marcion's radical revisions of the scriptures saw to that. That Marcion posed a significant threat to orthodox Christianity is evident in the number of Christian apologists who, over the course of two hundred years, felt impelled to write anti-Marcionite treatises: as mentioned earlier, Tertullian penned an extensive response to Marcion; Justin Martyr opposed him, as did Irenaeus, Hippolytus, Rhodo of Rome, Epiphanius, Bardesanes of Edessa, and many others.

5

THE OTHER GOSPELS

When the boy Jesus was five years old, he was playing at the ford of a rush-ing stream. He was collecting the flowing water into ponds and made the water instantly pure. He did this with a single command. He then made soft clay and shaped it into twelve sparrows. He did this on the sabbath day, and many other boys were playing with him. . . . So Joseph went there, and as soon as he spotted him, he shouted, "Why are you doing what's not permitted on the sabbath?"

But Jesus simply clapped his hands and shouted to the sparrows: "Be off, fly away, and remember me, you who are alive!" And the sparrows took off and flew away noisily.

—*THE INFANCY GOSPEL OF THOMAS* 2:1–3, 5–6
(SCHOLARS VERSION)

Some twenty-five million readers around the world have snapped up *The Da Vinci Code*, which makes it one of the best-selling novels of all time. There is no question that it is an ex-pertly paced and plotted thriller. Its heroine is gorgeous, its hero is smart and handsome, and its villains are frightening and charismatic. With its spectacular setting and its edge-of-the-seat chase scenes, the movie will undoubtedly break box-office records. But how does it stack up as a work of history?

The question is worth asking, because its author claims that all of its historical sources are genuine. And it's worth asking here, because its plot turns on some of the very "alternative Christianities" that are this book's subject. The short answer is that *The Da Vinci Code* is a work of fiction. Many of the events and documents that it refers to, such as the Council of Nicaea and the Gnostic gospels, are real (though the Priory of Sion, the ostensibly thousand-year-old society that plays such an important role in the book, was actually founded in the 1950s by a French con man), but they don't necessarily have the significance *The Da Vinci Code* attributes to them and certainly don't substantiate the supposedly vast conspiracy to suppress the truth about Jesus' relationship to Mary Magdalene that is at the heart of the novel.

Just as *The Da Vinci Code* declares, many gospels, with a great variety of messages, were written in the first three hundred years after Jesus' death. As we have seen in chapter 3, these gospels were not chapters of a fully formed book whose contents were set in stone, but a series of independent texts that a community would copy for themselves and perhaps pass on to others. For instance, here is a fragment from the Oxyrhynchus gospels, discovered in 1903 in the Egyptian city of the same name:

> When the scribes, Pharisees, and priests noticed him, they became incensed because he ate with sinners. But Jesus heard them and said, "The well don't need a doctor. And pray for your enemies, because the one who doesn't oppose you is on your side. The distant one today comes near tomorrow."

A local community might possess a Greek translation of some of the Old Testament, one or two gospels, maybe a letter or two of Paul, and a few other texts like this Oxyrhynchus fragment. Few churches had access to the complete New Testament (whatever a "complete" New Testament was deemed to be at the time) until Constantine commissioned them to be produced for the major churches of the empire in the fourth century.

A List of Known Gospels (Narrative or Sayings)

In the New Testament:

The Gospel of Mark

The Gospel of Matthew

The Gospel of Luke

The Gospel of John

In the Nag Hammadi Library:

The Gospel of Thomas

The Secret Book of James

The Dialogue of the Savior

The Gospel of Truth

The Gospel of Philip

The Gospel of the Egyptians

From other manuscript sources:

The Secret Gospel of Mark

The Gospel of Mary

The Gospel of the Savior

The Gospel of Peter

So a large variety of gospels (many of them markedly different in tone and content from the four canonical gospels), and even more gospel fragments, were circulating in the first few centuries of the Common Era. In later years, many of these communities—and their scriptures—would be looked upon with disfavor by the bishops, but in the beginning they were simply one form of Christianity among many others. The great variety of early gospels went with the great variety of early Christianities.

THE GOSPEL OF MARY

Portions of the *Gospel of Mary* survived in their original Greek in two fragmentary manuscripts dating from the third century. Portions of a fifth-century Coptic translation have also been recovered. The first of these was discovered in 1896, but it wasn't translated and published until the 1950s.

The Mary of the title is Mary Magdalene. No, this gospel doesn't confirm an earthly marriage between her and Jesus—far from it—but it opens an incredible window into the intellectual and spiritual world of the second century C.E., when it was originally composed. In the canonical gospels, it is Mary who learns of the resurrection and reports it to the other disciples. In this way she is the first apostle—the first to proclaim the good news that Jesus was risen. No small part to play in Christian revelation.

It should come as no surprise that there would be a gospel in Mary's name, but the gospel itself sheds light on why this idea is so controversial. After Mary shares her revelations with the apostles, Andrew objects that they are too strange to have come from Jesus. Peter chimes in, arguing that 1) Jesus would not have revealed such important teachings to a woman, and 2) her stature cannot be greater than that of the male apostles. Politics as usual.

Just as Paul called upon James, John, and Peter to adjudicate when he came into conflict with the other apostles, Levi (also known as Matthew) mediates between Mary and Peter here. Levi forces Peter to admit that it is his hot temper and pride that compels him to reject Mary; Peter concedes that her revelations are authentic.

So what in Mary's message was so strange to Andrew? There are three parts to Mary's gospel: a dialogue between Jesus and the disciples (unfortunately the first six pages of this are missing); Mary's own revelation; and the concluding argument among the disciples. From the little that's left of the opening dialogue, it seems that Jesus mostly talked about the nature of material and spiritual existence, maintaining that each will dissolve into its root. Sin, he said, came from mixing the spiritual with the material, which caused a disturbance in the believer.

After Jesus left the disciples, having commissioned them to proclaim the good news of the Kingdom of God, they "were distressed and wept exceedingly." Mary comforted them, turning their minds to spiritual things to refocus their attention. Then Peter asked her what special revelations Jesus had given to her alone. Unfortunately, four pages are missing from this section:

> Peter said to Mary, "My sister, we understand that the Savior loved you more than any other woman. Relate to us the sayings of the Savior that you know, but that we have never heard."
>
> Mary answered, "I will relate to you that which I remember that you do not know." So she began to tell them these sayings. "In a vision I saw the Lord, and I said to him, 'I saw you in a vision today, Lord.' He said to me, 'You are indeed blessed for not faltering at seeing me, because where your mind is, that is [where you will find] your treasure.' I said to him, 'Lord, how is it that a person who has a vision sees it—by means of the soul or by the spirit?' The Savior responded, 'Neither with the soul nor with the spirit does the one who sees a vision see it, but with the mind that mediates between these two.' "

With so many people experiencing visions of Jesus, and some even writing about them, the question of how such a vision is received became important. If visions indeed come from the mind, then it was quite possible for Mary to have a vision that was given only to her.

The second part of Mary's teaching presented information on the ascent of the soul from its entrapment in material existence to its liberation in the spiritual realm. The ascent involved such questioning as "Where are you going?" and "From where have you come?" Speculation about whether the soul achieves perfection in the body or only after death pervaded the religious and philosophical literature of the age; Mary's conversation with the risen Jesus addresses some of the hottest issues of the day. Her gospel also manifests in its own text the arguments that were already raging in the church about who would present the teachings of Jesus and what the contents of those teachings should be, foreshadowing its own eventual suppression.

THE GOSPEL OF THOMAS

"These are the mysterious sayings spoken by the living Jesus and recorded by Didymos Judas Thomas," the *Gospel of Thomas* begins. What an intriguing introduction: mysterious and secret words, a living Jesus, an apostolic recorder. Engaging with these sayings will bring immortality, not just understanding: "whoever discovers the interpretation of these sayings will never taste death." The *Gospel of Thomas* exemplifies an important dynamic of earliest Christianity: the impulse to collect the sayings of Jesus and promulgate them as the basis of individual and corporate meditation.

The *Gospel of Thomas* gathers together 114 brief aphorisms, parables, a few short narratives, and some dialogues with the disciples. There is no account of Jesus' birth, crucifixion, or resurrection, no healing stories; in short, none of the stuff that makes up the canonical gospels. What the gospel does feature in abundance is Jesus' unmediated voice, a voice that always speaks in the present tense, challenging readers and hearers to engage with the mind of God, to hear divine wisdom, and to apply this wisdom to their own life circumstances.

The earliest sayings probably date from Jesus' lifetime. The latest come from the period just before the publication of the gospel, around 110 C.E. Many seem to overlap the text that scholars believe Matthew and Luke must have drawn on to supplement their revision of the Gospel of Mark. This hypothetical "urtext" is commonly called Q, for the German word for "source" (*Quelle*).

The sayings collected in the *Gospel of Thomas* jump from subject to subject without apparent or obvious connections, but most of them are intended to challenge the norms of daily living. Jesus instructs his followers not to worry about food and clothing (Saying 36), not to perform pious acts such as fasting and almsgiving (Sayings 6 and 104), to hate their parents and siblings (Sayings 55 and 101), to lend money without expectation of interest or repayment (Saying 95); all in all, to adopt a thoroughly countercultural mode of life. No family values here! The only family that counted were those who were engaged with the living voice of the living Jesus.

Thomas's Jesus invited his followers to become a new kind of person—a single-minded person selected by God for special favor and grace (Sayings 23 and 49) and self-sufficient in understanding. "If you do not fast from the world, you will not find the [Father's] kingdom. If you do not observe the Sabbath as a Sabbath you will not see the Father" (Saying 27). He urged his listeners to leave the realm of those fated to die in order to live forever in the mind of God (Sayings 1, 11, 18, 19, 111), to join him in as intimate a communion as if they had gone into the bridal chamber together (Saying 75). "Whoever drinks from my mouth will become like me; I myself shall become that person, and the hidden things will be revealed to him" (Saying 108).

Not everyone can aspire to this level of religious commitment, and that was precisely what got the *Gospel of Thomas* into trouble. The creation of an elite group of people, empowered by an immediate apprehension of the divine mind, without the mediation of bishops and other clergy, threatened the dominant church. And so the church relegated it to the dustbin of history. It was a tremendous loss for Christians, then and now.

THE GOSPEL OF THE SAVIOR

About a decade ago an impromptu meeting was called at the annual meeting of the Society of Biblical Literature to encourage younger scholars who knew Coptic, a dialect of Egyptian into which many early Christian texts were translated, to edit and conserve documents from Egypt that had been stored in metal tins at the Berlin Egyptian Museum—some of them since the late nineteenth century. The documents were quickly disintegrating and in desperate need of preservation.

One volunteer discovered fragments of a previously unknown and unattested gospel. Only a few sheets of what appears to be a much longer text have survived relatively intact. Most of its pages are mere fragments, sometimes with only a letter or two that can be deciphered. Although the words "Jesus Christ" and "his disciples" do not appear in any part of the text, the gospel seems to be a discourse between the Savior and his followers.

It contains some surprising elements. The first is the Transfiguration, the episode where Moses and Elisha speak with Jesus on the mountain and his clothes become dazzling white. In this version it takes place *after* the crucifixion, not before, as in Matthew, Mark, and Luke (Mark 9:2–10; Matthew 17:1–9; Luke 9:28–36).

Second, the Savior addresses a long speech to the cross. At one point, he says, "You were eager for me, O cross; I also will be eager for you." Later the Savior again says: "A little longer, O cross, and that which is lacking is perfected, and that which is diminished is full. A little longer, O cross, and that which fell arises. A little longer, O cross, and all the *pleroma* is perfected." With these words, a shameful Roman instrument of torture is transformed into an instrument of salvation and restoration. The Savior eagerly embraces the cross as the means to achieve the perfection and salvation of the world.

Finally, Jesus gives the disciples a promise: "I will take you to heaven with me, and teach you." In this gospel, the theology of the resurrection involved transport to heaven, not the establishment of a missionary on earth.

Not much more can be said about the *Gospel of the Savior*. It is a treasure that has yet to come fully to light, but it dramatizes how much of early Christianity has been lost—and how much of what has been recovered can still disappear.

6

Feeling the Burn: Ascetic Christianity and the Quest for Bodily Purity

Once when a truly God-loving monk practiced interior prayer as he walked in the desert, two angels appeared and walked with him on either side of him. The God-loving monk, however, never paid them any attention, even for an instant, because he did not want to lose the better part. He remembered the apostle's words "neither angels, nor principalities, nor powers . . . shall be able to separate us from the love of God, which is in Christ Jesus our Lord" [Romans 8:38, 39].

—NILUS OF SINAI, *TEXTS ON PRAYER*, NO. 112

If while you are praying against some thought, you suddenly observe that it has dissipated quickly and without effort, study it to understand why this has happened so that you are not entrapped by it and, by fooling yourself, you become your own traitor.

—NILUS OF SINAI, *TEXTS ON PRAYER*, NO. 133

Fantasize with me a moment. Imagine that an ancient Christian ascetic climbs down from his pillar in the desert and gets fast-forwarded to a typical American shopping mall. You know the type: lots of clothing stores and restaurants, a gym or physical fitness center of some sort, and shops specializing in beauty products and weight loss. The usual.

Most early Christians, although they would have been shocked by the profligate displays of luxurious commercial products, would immediately understand where they were. After all, the mall is just a larger and more modern version of the agora, the ancient marketplace. The ancient ascetics, however, would especially be drawn to the gym, and to the beauty and weight loss clinics. Here they would see modern people doing almost exactly the same things as they did, but for radically different reasons.

Modern people go to gyms in order to recast their body into something tight, supple, fit, and healthy. The well-toned body cries out beauty, hard work, self-respect, and the joy of recasting flabby and homely flesh into something the culture regards as beautiful and youthful. The dieters at the weight loss centers have a similar goal; they strive to become different people through their disciplined perseverance: thin, newly attractive, no longer weighed down by fat. And the cosmetics and ointments that the beauty centers sell—they too re-create people in a new and more beautiful image.

The ancient ascetic would understand these modern practices because they correlate with his own. Pummeling themselves with fasts, prostrations, and prayer, ascetics created new bodies for themselves that were tight, supple, fit—and holy. Fasting dried out their bodies, making them more suitable vessels for the Holy Spirit, less subject to worldly desires. Their disciplined exertions led them to closer communion, if not union, with God. And they undertook rigorous cosmetic regimes, too—to accomplish precisely the opposite of what people seek today. If modern people pamper their flesh, the Christian ascetics punished it, restricting their bathing to a bare minimum and rubbing ashes not only on their bodies but into their food.

If modern ascetics hope that their efforts will be rewarded with more and better sex and higher social status—carnal goals all—the ancients worked their bodies to make them godly. The ends differ starkly; the means are strikingly similar.

This section introduces two varieties of asceticism that were common in ancient Christianity. Neither of them was ever declared to be heretical, and though rare, versions of them still survive today. The established church didn't have to stamp these movements out; they simply lost their popularity.

WHO WERE THE "CONTINENTS" (AKA ENCRATITES)? The modern "just say no" movements have an ancient equivalent. The "continents" or the "self-controlled" (in Greek *enkrateia*, hence "Encratites") would have agreed with their modern counterparts about sex and alcohol. Some things are so dangerous that they should be avoided altogether. In addition to being considered immoral, premarital sex may lead to unwanted pregnancies and contribute to the spread of sexually transmitted diseases. Likewise, drinking or taking drugs can lead to death by overdose or other mishaps. Neither of these consequences pleases parents or society.

The Encratites felt the same way. Sex and alcohol involved men and women in social and cultural circumstances that distracted them from God, so they renounced them altogether.

Their religious discipline revolved around celibacy, the rejection of marriage, and the regulation of food, especially wine.

The so-called "family values" celebrated by many Christians today were not so obvious to some earlier Christians. These self-controlled and continent Christians thoroughly rejected social and political marriages of the sort that lead to families in favor of "spiritual marriages," which had no sexual component at all. Men and women, even some who were married and had raised families prior to their conversion to Christianity, renounced their sexual relationships in order to live "as angels," neither male nor female, in spiritual relationships. These spiritually married people devoted themselves to the production of spiritual children: the virtues, acts of mercy, unceasing prayer, and the work of the church. They would set up a household just like other households, but their houses were dedicated to the development of their spiritual lives. Obviously sometimes these "spiritual marriages" fell into carnality. Many bishops derided these relationships as far too dangerous for the common person and encouraged people either to marry and engage in licit sexual relationships or to enter the monastic communities that had begun to blossom at that same period. The spiritual marriages occurred primarily in urban contexts, while monasteries grew up in mostly rural or isolated environments. We will learn more about monastic Christianity in the next chapter.

A DIFFERENT KIND OF ROMANCE NOVEL

Most of what we know about the Encratites comes from a fascinating body of literature: the early Christian novels. Yes, I said novels. These novels, usually categorized under the rubric of the "apocryphal acts of the apostles," relate stories about the missionary work that the apostles undertook after the resurrection of Jesus. They are replete with miraculous events. The apostles raise the dead, heal the sick, convert the recalcitrant. The power of God is so great that even fresh converts can accomplish the same miraculous deeds.

The Best-Known "Christian Novels"

The Acts of Paul and Thecla

The Acts of Andrew

The Acts of John

The Acts of Peter

The Acts of Thomas

The Acts of Peter and the Twelve Apostles

The Acts of Peter and Paul

The Acts of Andrew and Matthew

The Acts of Peter and Andrew

The Acts of Paul and Andrew

The Acts of Philip

The apostles and their converts performed these miracles to show that their God was superior to all other gods. In the *Acts of John*, for example, John went to the famous sanctuary of the Roman goddess Artemis at Ephesus (in modern Turkey) and by prayer smashed all the idols and holy places to prove to the people who were watching that his God was stronger and better than theirs. Of course, they were all converted.

But the apostles' contests with the Roman gods were about more than brute force. The Christian God demanded that all social relationships and all familial relationships be redefined. Now that their bodies were temples of the Holy Spirit, the newly baptized were expected to remain pure, unmarried, chaste, and undefiled. The will to persevere as a virgin showed forth the majesty of their God as much as any act of healing or destruction.

That message of chastity and virginity surprised people then as much as it does now. Listen to Paul's reworking of the beatitudes in the *Acts of Paul and Thecla* (2:5):

> Blessed are the pure in heart; they shall see God.
> Blessed are they that keep their bodies from sex; they
>   will be a temple of God.
> Blessed are the continents; God will speak to them.
> Blessed are the world-renouncers; they please God.
> Blessed are those who have wives as if they were single;
>   they will inherit God. . . .
>
> Blessed are the ones who have kept their baptism pure;
>   they will certainly rest with the Father and the
>   Son. . . .
> Blessed are the virginal bodies; they really please God
>   and will forfeit the reward of their self-control.

Upon hearing this message the sainted Thecla, a very popular female apostle of the early church, vowed that she would never marry and became a Christian instead. Rejecting her arranged marriage with Thamyris, she set off to become an itinerant missionary like Paul, preaching fidelity to Christ through virginity alone.

For the Encratites the purity of their bodies, their undefiled state, formed the basis of their power. The chaste could keep their minds on God without the distraction of raising children, or keeping a household, or catering to a spouse. Real power consisted in purging the body of its carnal desires in order to become a habitation for God alone. Power and chastity went hand in hand.

Women in particular play an important role in these stories. Wives who have rejected their husbands form communities where they can dedicate themselves to prayer. Renouncing social status and wealth, they exchange worldly for spiritual power.

The underpinning to this reversal rested in the contrast between permanent and impermanent things. The riches of the Roman nobility—gold, fine clothing, large households filled with slaves and client servants—were things that would eventually corrode and die. The things of the Spirit of God, however, were eternal. Husbands and households die, but Jesus will always live, so these women took on Jesus as their eternal, spiritual spouse.

In the following exerpt from the *Acts of Thomas* (section 123), Mygdonia, who has rejected her fiancé now that she has been converted to a life of continence, explains the theology of her marriage to Jesus. I begin with the conversation that leads into the theology:

> Coming close to her, Charisius entreated her again, saying: "Please listen to me and I will grieve no longer. Do

you remember the day that you first saw me? Tell me truthfully, was I not more beautiful to you than Jesus is to you now?"

Mygdonia answered, "That was then, this is now. That was a beginning, but this time is an ending. That time was passing, but this time is eternal. That pleasure was transient, but this pleasure lasts forever. That time [was marked by the passing] of day and night, but this time [consists of] day without night. You saw the earthly marriage that passed away, but this marriage lasts forever. That sexual relationship was full of corruption, but this intimacy is full of eternal life. Those bridal attendants are mere passing human men and women, but these [with Jesus] will remain with me forever. That bridal chamber would be disassembled, but this bridal chamber lasts forever. You spread that bed with blankets, but this one is spread with faith and love. You are a bridegroom who will die and dissolve, but Jesus, the true bridegroom, will live immortally forever. Your bridal gifts consist of money and clothes that age, but this bridal gift [of Jesus] consists of living words that will never pass away."

Withdrawal from society opened the possibility of doing something really new, really different. But the way of life that these Christian novels celebrated was just as alternative for many Christians as it was for the Romans. Not every Christian considered virginity to be the normative state after baptism; not all Christians expected their religious leaders to perform miracles. The Encratite way of life seemed extreme; it was held

in suspicion as vaguely heretical or dualistic. The Romans simply thought it weird and strange. Some Christians, I am sure,
agreed with them.

The one way that these novels might be genuinely heretical
is in how they image Jesus. Very often the women of these Acts
would look at the apostle and see Jesus himself sitting there. To
those who needed to see an old man, Jesus presented himself as
an old man; to those who needed a young boy, Jesus appeared
as a young boy; to those who needed to see an angelic being,
Jesus would appear as a bright angel. Later on the bishops
would find such a polymorphous Christology to be dangerous,
but at the time that these novels were written such fluidity of
identity made for interesting plot twists.

These novels were the most popular form of early Christian
literature. They formed generations of early Christian women
and children, introducing them to new ways of living. Their
early readers may have also read them as liberating fantasies.
While they remained locked behind the social requirements of
households both Christian and Roman, these novels gave them
a glimpse of a completely different way of life.

WHAT WAS SOLITARY MONASTICISM?

There is a circus sideshow aspect to many of the early Christian
ascetic movements—and not just because some of them were
deeply strange and bizarre. The circus, after all, calls day-to-day
life into question, offering in its place a vision of an alternative
world, filled with unfamiliar animals and unexpected events.

People walk on wires that are suspended high above the ground, happy- and sad-looking clowns perform both to entertain and to teach lessons about life. So it was for some of the solitary monks and ascetics of the early church. They lived on the very edge of society, if not completely outside of it, commenting on the world as they saw it from their unique perspective.

Two kinds of monasticism emerged in the early church: cenobitic and eremitical. The cenobitic monks formed small communities; the eremitical monks lived independently but were gathered very loosely around a charismatic teacher. The eremitical monks tended to be the most outrageous and theatrical monks of the early church. Both kinds of monasticism have survived into the modern day, but the eremitical is much rarer than it was.

Eremites were women and men who withdrew from all social relationships, including the church, in order to spend all their time alone with God. St. Anthony, the famous Egyptian hermit, set the course: at first he withdrew to the cemetery outside his small Egyptian village; then he went farther into the desert; and finally he walled himself into a building in the deep inner desert so that he could be completely alone.

Anthony withdrew in order to contend with demons, his interior thoughts made physically manifest in his contest with evil forces. Actually he wasn't all that alone. His followers gathered about a day's walk away so they could provide for him. Sometimes they gathered together on a Saturday evening for prayer and conversation, maybe even a liturgy or two. But this was not always the case. Hermits were recluses; they did not want the company of any other monk, nor of any church official. Mostly

The Eight Monastic Deadly Sins

These sins were considered "deadly" because they thwarted the spiritual impulse and caused a kind of deadening of the soul. Usually we hear about seven deadly sins, but the hermit monks of Egypt, Syria, France, and Italy actually had eight deadly sins against which they fought. The eighth, called *acedia* in Greek, was so hard to translate that it was simply easier to leave it out. But here are the eight and their significance:

Gluttony. Since monks fast so much, the desire for food can really be debilitating. Too much food—or comfort of any sort—hinders an ascetic's progress.

Lust. Living alone, constantly attending to one's fantasies, an ascetic can easily succumb to lust. Lust can impel the ascetic to leave the monastery or hermitage altogether, or, just as bad, to indulge in masturbation. Impurity as an act and lust as a desire both caused serious problems and the ascetic needed to fight both assiduously.

Greed. This is the material side of lust, when the ascetic is overwhelmed by intense desires for such creature comforts as a soft bed, or books, or a better place to live. These desires for things try to fill a void that only prayer and meditation should fill. Things get in the way of the one truth, which is that God should be the ascetic's only true possession—everything else has no significance.

Sadness. An ascetic could easily become melancholy living alone, lost in his or her own thoughts, living a subsistence existence far away from friends, family, and others. The ascetic has to fight the tendency toward sadness by envisioning the company of ascetic saints, angels, and even God himself.

Anger. Spending so much time by themselves, ascetics can begin to perseverate about all the people and events that did them harm. Since they have no means of reconciliation, they can easily become mired in anger and frustration. Anger prevents the ascetic from making progress toward holiness of life.

Acedia is a name for the tediousness of religious striving. It is also called the noonday sin, because when the sun is high in the sky the heat can make the hermit feel the tedium of praying and fasting all the more acutely. Time often seems to stand still for the ascetic—prayer becomes frustrating, habitual patterns become more stubborn, spiritual progress feels illusory. Such feelings can be fatal to the religious life.

Vainglory. In a sense this is the opposite of acedia. Here the ascetic fills up the self with a sense of accomplishment and comes to rely not upon divine assistance, but upon his or her own gifts and accomplishments. Vainglory puffs up the self to the point that it can no longer relate to God, thus ceasing to strive for holiness.

Pride. Pride in progress leads to boasting about it, or thinking that holiness has already been achieved. This is a very dangerous spiritual state that can lead the ascetic to fall into deeper sin. Pride takes the glory away from God and attributes it to the self.

they stayed alone in order to pray to God and to do battle with God's enemies who lodged themselves within them.

The following selections from the *Sayings of the Desert Masters* are intended to startle, confront, engage, fascinate, and otherwise disturb normal patterns of thinking. They reveal the uncompromising integrity of the hermit's way of life.

> Father Joseph went to visit Father Lot. Joseph said to him: "Holy Father, as much as I am able I perform my ascetical duties: I pray a little; I fast a little; I pray and meditate in silence as much as I can; and I cleanse my thoughts according to my ability. What more do I need to do?" Lot got up and stretched out his hands to heaven, and his fingers became ten candles aflame, and he said to Joseph, "If you really want to, you can become entirely fire."

> The holy mother Syncletica said, "When the unrighteous turn to God they first struggle and experience difficult work; afterward they are filled with unspeakable happiness. It is just like a person who is kindling a fire. First they have smoke that pains their eyes and they cry; but afterward, they get what they want. So it is with us hermits. It is written, 'Our God is a consuming fire' [Deuteronomy 4:24] and that requires that we kindle the divine fire within us with hard work and tears."

> A famous hermit came to talk to Father Pastor about lofty things. But Pastor turned his head away from the hermit, and the hermit left him greatly saddened. Pastor's student asked him why he did not want to talk with such

a famous person who had a great reputation in his own country. Pastor replied that his visitor came to talk about lofty things, but that he was just an earthly being. Pastor said, "If he had asked me about the temptations of the soul, I could have given him some advice; but I am stupid when it comes to lofty things." The famous hermit overheard this and was deeply moved to learn from the old man, so he said to Pastor: "Holy Father, what can I do? The temptations of my soul rule my life." Then they conversed for a very long time, and the famous hermit then said, "This is really love's way."

A younger brother asked an older hermit, saying, "I don't know what to do. I do not seem to act like a monk. I eat, drink, and sleep without discipline. I have terribly wicked thoughts. I'm really troubled and cannot seem to concentrate, moving from one task and one thought to another." The older hermit said, "Stay in your hermit's cell and do not be troubled about how little you do. For doing little is equal to the great value of what Father Anthony did on the holy mountain. By staying put in your cell, sitting in the Name of God, guarding your thoughts carefully, you will find the same joy that Anthony found."

WHO WERE THE *BOSKOI*?

The *boskoi* were the cattle ascetics. No, they did not eat beef. The word *boskoi* means "grazers." True to their name, they acted like cattle, crawling naked on their hands and knees and eating grass as if they were animals. Sound strange? Well, it was, but there was a method to their seeming madness. The grazers understood that the world had gone far astray from that which God had intended when he created it. The garden of Eden had been a natural world in which all the parts cohered. Humans had not been at the center of this primal paradise; in fact, God created man exactly as he had made all the other animals. But when Adam sinned, the world changed. The only way to undo the work of Adam was to return to the world as it was before his fall. So back to the animal state, back to being grazers. The *boskoi*'s grazing restored the world to its pristine purity.

WHO WERE THE STYLITES?

The Stylites were the high-wire acts of the ancient ascetic circus. These holy men climbed onto high pillars (*stylos* means "pillar" in Greek) and lived on them for years at a time. The pillars were topped with a small platform that provided just enough space to stand and pray, and maybe to squat for a while to rest. Sometimes the pillar was big enough to hold a tiny house that protected its resident saint from the blistering heat of the summer and the wet and cold of the winter, but not all of them used those houses.

The Stylites, too, had a reason for what they did. Perched upon their pillars, these saints saw themselves as suspended halfway between heaven and earth. They had ascended to a place that was separate from the world and above it, if not as high as heaven. Since they literally saw the world from a loftier vantage, they brought a divine perspective to human affairs. Rulers and common people alike came to them to seek counsel, for help in reconciling with their enemies, and for prayers for healing and forgiveness. The pillar saints provided access to the heavenly graces; they modeled what life would look like for the angels and those perfect few who could sustain their ascetic efforts. It was far from an easy life, but they embraced its harshness as an opportunity to do penance on behalf of the sinful world and its people.

One monk, Symeon the Stylite, stood for so long that his leg became gangrenous. His response was to write a hymn in praise of this noble limb, which had expended itself in the service of the man of God.

WHO WERE THE "FOOLS FOR CHRIST"?

On the next day, which was a Sunday, he took nuts, and entering the church at the beginning of the liturgy, he threw the nuts and put out the candles. When they hurried to run after him, he went up to the pulpit, and from there he pelted the women with nuts. With great trouble, they chased after him, and while he was going out, he overturned the pastry chefs, who nearly beat him to death. Seeing himself crushed by the blows, he said to himself, "Poor Symeon, if things like this keep happening, you won't live a week in these people's hands."

—LEONTIUS OF NEAPOLIS, *THE LIFE OF SYMEON THE FOOL**

*Derek Krueger, *Symeon the Holy Fool: Leontius's* Life *and the Late Antique City* (Berkeley: University of California Press, 1996), p. 151.

At the other end of the spectrum were the fools for Christ. Like circus clowns, these monks did crazy things that no one would expect from a monk or an ascetic. They took Paul's injunction that he was a fool (1 Corinthians 4:10) literally and imitated his foolishness as a sign of grace. They openly disdained the rites and ceremonies conducted by the privileged clergy. They would often live among the most unclean of the city—prostitutes, theater performers, and those living on the ancient streets. They ate large quantities of beans and expressed their flatulence in public and in church buildings. They ate garbage and they seldom bathed. They often defecated and urinated in public.

Their point, as they understood it, was a simple one. The ways and wisdom of God look foolish to humans (1 Corinthians 1:21), so in order to understand God, humans must become fools. One cannot both know God and act normally. That is impossible.

Although these itinerant fools do not appear very often in the modern period, they have been known throughout the history of Christianity. They tend to emerge whenever the church becomes too rich and powerful or when the Christians identify too strongly with social and political power. The modern Russian *Way of a Pilgrim*, immortalized in the novel *Franny and Zooey*, is the most popular example.

WHO WERE THE VAGRANT MONKS?

These monks embraced a life of poverty with intense fasting and permanent homelessness. They wandered from city to city throughout the Christian Roman Empire, gathering around the martyrs' shrines and begging for money and food—not for themselves, but for the poor, who were energized by their charismatic presence. They, too, had a theological point to make.

These vagrant monks literally represented Christ to the community. They imitated Christ's poverty, his wandering way of life, his devotion to the poor, and his association with sinners and outcasts. They were very holy. They were also very popular. And that was the problem. They posed a serious danger to the church hierarchy and to the governments that they implicitly challenged; eventually they inspired legislation requiring all monks to be connected with a community.

All of these solitary ascetics displayed a radical reliance upon God alone and made no secret of their rabid hatred for a social, political, and even ecclesiastical world that paid more attention to property and propriety than to God. Their outrageous and provocative behavior challenged the rest of society and the church to acknowledge the clash between a stable social order and the Kingdom of God.

7

Holy Rollers and Sacred Terrorists

The king ordered the maidservants to be brought along, and he addressed them as well: "You have seen your masters and mistresses, as well as your relatives, die an evil death because they refused to renounce Christ and the cross. But do you spare yourselves; listen to me, deny Christ and the cross. Then you shall become free women, and I will give you away to freeborn husbands." But they replied, "Far be it from us to deny Christ and the cross; far be it from us to remain alive after our masters and companions have died; no, we along with them and like them, will die for the sake of Christ. Far be it from us to consent to you and accept your proposition." When the king saw that they could not be persuaded to deny Christ, he ordered that they be brought to the wadi, or ravine, and put to death there. This was carried out, and they were all crowned by the sword.

—ACCOUNT OF A MARTYRDOM IN PERSIA,
SIMEON OF BETH ARSHAM, SECOND LETTER*

All religions have their "holy rollers," those faithful whose enthusiasm pushes them to the edge of propriety and even to the edge of society. Often these charismatic enthusiasts attract

*Sebastian Brock and Susan Ashbrook Harvey, *Holy Women of the Syrian Orient* (Berkeley: University of California Press, 1987), p. 109.

large crowds of people who seem somehow dissatisfied, or maybe even bored, with the steady and rational religion of the majority.

Ancient religion was no exception. The priests of Cybele, the mother goddess of the ancient Near East, worked themselves into ecstatic transports in which they'd castrate themselves. Some ancient Christians also bordered on the crazed. Imagine walking into a Christian assembly in Corinth. Paul describes how people would eat and drink and even get drunk (1 Corinthians 11:21–22)! The participants spoke in strange languages, prophecy abounded; the scene was so chaotic that Paul had to intervene, insisting that they take turns praying and singing. This epitomizes enthusiastic, charismatic Christianity, a tradition that still lives on today, as a visit to any Pentecostal church in your neighborhood will confirm.

WHO WERE THE MONTANISTS?

Walking into a Montanist church would have been like walking into a contemporary Pentecostal church—except it would have been filled with radical, leftist feminists. People all around you would look like they were in a trance, their faces tilted back, pointing toward heaven, their eyes focused on another world. You would feel the emotion in the air.

Woman after woman, then man after man, would channel words from God, while the others listened attentively. "I am your God and I am with you. Turn to me only!" A woman presiding at the worship service might proclaim: "I am driven away as a wolf from sheep. I am not a wolf. I am word and spirit

and power." The sermon, preached by a woman, would casti-
gate the church for its refusal to bend to the spirit, for its cap-
tivation by social norms, for its discrimination against the
women and the prophets of God. Charismatic chaos and
women's liberation melded together. That is the spirit of Montanism.

Montanus, the male founder of this Christian movement,
began to prophesy in Phrygia, in Asia Minor (modern Turkey)
sometime around 170 C.E. Reaching back into the Pauline
Epistles, especially the letters to the Corinthians, Montanus
called forth a vision of a church renewed—filled with the Holy
Spirit of God, alive with fresh prophecy, and eagerly awaiting
the imminent return of Christ. Montanus was a new Paul. His
prophecy, like Paul's ministry, gathered the elect into a spirit-
filled communion of people preparing for the eagerly awaited
and dreaded Day of the Lord, when Jesus would return to establish the Kingdom of God on earth.

But Montanus's expectations were read through Jesus'
promise in the Gospel of John to send a Paraclete (John
14:15–17), a Holy Spirit that acts as an advocate, comforter,
and divine intercessor: "If you love me, preserve my laws, and I
will ask the Father and he will give you another Paraclete that
will be with you until the end of time. [It is] the Spirit of truth,
which this world is not capable of receiving because it neither
sees it nor knows it; but you know it because it dwells in you
and will live in you."

Two women prophets joined Montanus in creating and sup-
porting this early Christian renewal movement: Prisca and
Maximilla. It was Maximilla who prophesied: "I am driven
away as a wolf from sheep. I am not a wolf. I am word and spirit

and power." The two prophetesses channeled the divine voice through their bodies, which were purified by rigorous fasting and prayer.

The ancient world outside Christianity knew and valued women prophets. The oracle of the god Apollo at both Delphi and Didyma had had women prophets, and there were many other shrines where oracles could be consulted and where women mediated the message. We seem to find the same dynamic in the Pauline letters. Some women could pray and speak in a prophetic voice in the worship service (1 Corinthians 11:5). And certainly Paul does not prohibit women from receiving the gift of prophecy (1 Corinthians 12:4–11). The ancient world was more interested and concerned about the purity and moral stature of the person than about gender when it came to speaking a word from God to the people. These Montanist women stood in a long line of women prophets.

It is not easy to describe the Montanists. They were apocalyptic because they awaited the cataclysmic return of Christ to the New Jerusalem, which they expected to occur at Pepuza in Phrygia (modern Turkey). They were ecstatic because they sought to displace themselves and their own consciousness in order to be filled with divine utterance. They were prophetic because they pronounced severe judgments on the current world and its mores. And they were ascetic because they demanded a high level of bodily purity, which they achieved by fasting and sexual abstinence, before they could be worthy to have the divine indwelling. The Montanists had everything a religious rigorist could possibly want.

The Montanists understood their new prophecy as a renewal movement for an increasingly decadent church, which had assimilated itself to the social and political customs of the day. Their prophecy sought to bridge the old world of charismatic prophecy and the new world that would come with the Second Coming of Christ. Their bodies, filled with the Spirit of God and speaking God's voice, literally created the bridge.

WHAT DID THE MONTANISTS BELIEVE?

Most of the evidence comes from their enemies, but we can make some educated guesses. Their enemies conceded that the Montanists did not stray from the dominant church's teachings about basic doctrines, nor did they vary from its sacramental and hierarchical system. They were not heretics in that sense. What disturbed the church fathers was their exceptional rigor and enthusiasm.

Following Pauline teaching in 1 Corinthians 7:1–16, the Montanists considered virginity to be the only bodily state that could be consecrated fully to God. Those who were already married could remain married, as Paul had suggested, but widowed, separated, or divorced people were forbidden to remarry. The solitary state, unpolluted by sexual intercourse, provided the ideal home for the divine Spirit. As mentioned earlier, the Montanists also fasted intensely.

Following Pauline practices, the Montanists ordained women to holy orders as deacons, presbyters (priests), and bishops. If you believe most of the leaders of major Christian denominations today, you would think that women's leadership in the church is something new. Nothing could be further from the truth. Just a quick glance at Paul's greetings to people in Rome

(Romans 16) shows that Phoebe was a deacon, Prisca and Mary coworkers, Junia an apostle, and Tryphena a worker for the Lord, not to mention Julia and Olympas, who were good friends. To Paul's witness can be added the dogged witness of Mary Magdalene to the resurrection of Jesus in all the canonical gospels, as well as the ministry of other women who followed Jesus from the beginning (Mark 15:40–41). Women not only played an important role in extending the church to their households, but also provided vital and significant leadership to the church throughout the early period. The Montanists carried on this tradition.

The Montanists' rigorous faith did not admit of any compromises. If a member of their church succumbed to Roman pressure to acknowledge their gods and make sacrifices, they would not be permitted to rejoin the church. They were prime targets for martyrdom and persecution by the Romans and they welcomed their fate.

The early church had often stipulated that prophets should never request money or support. The Montanists' opponents accused them of violating this rule—of collecting funds, making provisions for receiving gifts, and even of paying their clergy and prophets salaries. Apparently this was true. By the time of Montanism, Jesus' injunctions to poverty had long since been reinterpreted to allow the dominant church to accumulate wealth and property. The Montanists, who maintained the clerical hierarchy of the dominant church, also followed its general administrative practices. Their fervency for reform did not extend to their church's structure.

Finally, the Montanists believed in prophecy. Prophecy in the early church did not mean predicting future events—that is

a decidedly modern view. Ancient prophets spoke on behalf
of the deity, delivering messages from God to the people.
Prophecy revealed God's will and God's direction for those
who would listen. Sometimes the prophet's revelations carried
a threat of action should the people not follow God's will, and
in this way the prophet predicted the future. But mostly the
prophets simply delivered God's message.

More than anything else, this was the cause of their argument with the dominant church. The Montanists believed that
their minds and bodies were filled with the divine presence
when they prophesied. The Montanists did not experience
themselves as messengers or speakers on behalf of God as the
orthodox theologians argued, but as human and bodily vessels
through which God channeled his voice and spoke directly to
the people. "I am the Father, the Word, and the Paraclete,"
Didymus the Blind quoted a Montanist proclaiming (*On the
Trinity* 3:41). Epiphanius, in *Medicine Chest Against All Heresies,* quoted two more Montanist prophecies: "I am the Lord,
the Omnipotent God, who has descended into a human" and
"I, the Lord, have come—not an angel, not even an ambassa-
dor" (XLVIII.1).

Obviously the leadership of the church could not have people claiming to channel the divine voice directly. They insisted
that true prophets had a vision of God and then related it, or
heard God speak and then reported his words to others. For
the orthodox church, the human person could never fully represent the divine. And so the Montanists eventually were excommunicated.

The Montanist rigor and purity attracted not only common
people, but also intellectuals and theologians. The famous North

African Latin theologian Tertullian (160–225) converted to
the movement and wrote energetically from a Montanist perspective. The Montanist churches survived well into the seventh century C.E.

WHO WERE THE DONATISTS
AND THE CIRCUMCELLIONS?

Violence and terrorism abounded in the ancient world. The
Roman leaders used crucifixion as an instrument of social and
political control; Roman citizens were fascinated by the bloody
spectacle provided by their circuses, where various political and
social enemies were pitted against each other as gladiators or
fought to preserve themselves against the attack of wild animals. And not all the violence was inflicted by the Romans.
Some of their subjects gave as good as they got.

The parallels between ancient and modern religious terrorism are sobering. The Circumcellions of the Donatist movement, whom we will next study, bear a disturbing resemblance
to today's Islamic "living bombs," people who destroy themselves in order to perpetrate violence against their religious
enemies. Then as now, martyrdom, violence, and religious enthusiasm create a deadly mix.

But before we get to the Donatists and the Circumcellions,
we need to start with the Great Persecution by the Roman
emperor Diocletian (who reigned from 284 to 305 C.E.). Diocletian grieved the increasing neglect of traditional Roman religion, particularly in the provinces. His solution was twofold:
to legislate adherence to traditional Roman religious practices,

and to punish and destroy the people and their institutions who most opposed it, namely the Christians.

On February 24, 303, Diocletian promulgated his first edict against the Christians. The practice of Christianity was outlawed: church buildings were ordered to be destroyed, and sacred books confiscated and burned. A year later Diocletian added the stipulation that Christians had to offer incense to the Roman gods or lose their lives.

This persecution created three categories of Christians. The martyrs refused to comply with the imperial edicts and were killed. The confessors also refused to comply with the imperial edicts and were condemned to death, but for whatever reason their sentences were never carried out. Christians regarded these first two categories as venerable and holy—they were understood to have a special anointing of the Holy Spirit, a special charism, that bestowed upon them extraordinary spiritual rights and privileges. They were permitted to forgive sins and celebrate the sacraments without ordination in the prisons where they were held.

The third category was the *traditores,* those who handed over the scriptures to be burned, or gave the names of other Christians to the Roman officials, or cooperated in any way with the Roman persecution. Needless to say, they were despised. *Traditores* literally means "the ones who handed over"; the term became synonymous with "traitor."

After the Great Persecution subsided in 305 with Diocletian's death, a majority of bishops concluded that it was necessary to reconcile with these traitors in order to restore the church and begin its reconstruction. These bishops maintained that *traditores* could repent of their sinful action and, after a suitable period of penance, participate in church life again without shame or guilt. The Donatists were of a very different opinion.

In 311 Caecilian was consecrated Catholic bishop of Carthage in North Africa. One of his consecrators, however, had been a *traditor*. To many in North Africa, this invalidated his ordination. In 313 Donatus (d. 355) was consecrated as a rival bishop to Caecilian. The Donatist movement takes its name from him.

The Donatists believed that the church exists only for those who have kept themselves faithful to God. Their church was a communion of the holy and saved, not a hospital for sinners. If the Catholic Church was willing to reconcile with traitors, the Donatists would not. Those who had renounced their faith by collaborating with the persecutors of the Christians had permanently put themselves beyond the pale.

The Donatists went one step further, however. They argued that so long as the Catholic Church allowed reconciled clergy to function as religious leaders, none of their sacraments would be valid. Not only did the Donatists hold the Catholic clergy liable for their own actions, they held them liable for those who had consecrated them. Poor Caecilian was not himself a sinner. He had never handed over the scriptures or betrayed anyone to the authorities. But one of the bishops who consecrated him had, so for the Donatists Caecilian too bore the stain of his consecrator's sin. The Donatists had no room for gray, only black and white. So long as the Catholic Church included *traditores*, no matter how penitent they were, then the Catholic Church was invalid. Any baptism performed by any priest or bishop who was not a Donatist had to be renewed and revalidated by the rituals of the Donatist priests and bishops.

St. Augustine of Hippo (354–430 C.E.) on the Donatists
It is not often that we can hear from both sides, but the following passage captures the heat of the argument between the Donatists and Rome. The quotation is from one of Augustine's three books answering *The Letters of Petilian, the Donatist* (Book II, 32, 72–73). (Petilian was the Donatist bishop of Cirta in North Africa.)

Petilian had written:

> Even though there is only one baptism, it is consecrated in three grades. John baptized without naming the Trinity, as he himself says, "I baptize you with water for repentance; but the one that comes after me is mightier than I am. I am not worthy to tie his shoes. But he will baptize you with the Holy Spirit and with fire" (Matthew 3:11). Christ bestowed the Holy Spirit, as written in the Bible, "He breathed upon them and said, 'Receive the Holy Spirit' " (John 20:22). Then the Comforter himself came down upon the disciples as a fire burning in tongues of flames. . . . But you, persecutor, do not have the repenting water, because you have the power not of John who was murdered, but the power of the murderer Herod. That is why you, traitor, do not have the Holy Spirit of Christ, because Christ did not hand over others to die, but he himself was handed over. For you traitors the fire burning your spirit is the fire of a hell full of life— that fire which consuming with hungry tongues of flames will be capable of burning your limbs eternally without consuming them.

Punic language and knew nothing of the Latin language of their rulers.

Declaring war against all enemies of the true church, these roving bands used clubs, which they called "Israel" (for whatever reason) to beat their opponents—Catholic landowners and clergy, debt and tax collectors, and anyone else who represented wealth and privilege. Their slogan was "Praise God," a phrase that must have inspired fear and trembling in the Catholic faithful.

The Circumcellions avidly embraced martyrdom. When they weren't attacking their coreligionists, they sought out and attended pagan rites in order to renounce them, hoping to provoke the Romans to make them martyrs. Although the Donatists officially rejected many of their activities, the Circumcellions persisted as a strong military force in support of the Donatist clergy and church—indeed, the Circumcellions kept the Donatist reverence for martyrdom alive.

I began this section by comparing the Donatists and Circumcellions with the fundamentalist Islamic clerics and martyr cells of today. That comparison certainly stands up, and Christians would do well to remember it before pointing their condemning fingers at all of Islam. But another parallel between the Donatists and the modern churches should be noticed as well. Almost without exception, modern Christian denominations have fallen into the Donatist heresy, condemning sinners of many sorts as unworthy of ordination and attempting to separate themselves from them. The major issues that divide the "pure" from the "impure" today include abortion, homosexuality, and the role of women in the church.

It's worth remembering that the Donatist conception of the

church as the preserve of the saved alone lost out. The Catholic Church of the period won by offering reconciliation—by welcoming back into its fold those whom it and others considered sinful, and by arguing that the sacraments remain valid even if the clergy who are performing them are sinful.

The rigorist Donatists and the Circumcellions preserved themselves for many years, surviving long into the seventh century. Both their vigorous dedication to purity and the negative example of their rejection of compromise would have a lasting influence on the Church.

8

CHALLENGES TO CHRISTIANITY
FROM THE ROMAN WORLD

But if there is ignorance, and learning does not exist in the soul of a person, then the incurable passions persist in the soul. And additional evil comes the passions in the form of an incurable sore. And the sore constantly gnaws at the soul, and through it the soul produces worms from the evil and stinks. But God is not the cause of these things, since he sent knowledge and learning to human beings.

—*ASCLEPIUS* 66:13–25[*] NHLE

It has been argued that Christianity succeeded in the ancient world because the local Roman religions were boring and uninteresting. Not so! Religions of every sort thrived in the ancient period. Not only did they thrive, but they competed with one another for adherents. The religious environment was literally a marketplace.

Picture your neighborhood supermarket. Very likely it's part of a complex that also includes a pharmacy, a bank, a video store, an electronics outlet, and a music depot. Children stand at the door selling things to raise money for their schools; per-

[*]With minor modifications by author.

haps someone is handing out leaflets for a cause. The Roman and Greek marketplace, the agora, functioned in exactly the same way, except that philosophers and religious adherents would also set up stalls. So the ancient person would bank, shop, and hear about different religious and philosophical traditions all in the same place, at the same time, week after week. The competition was fierce. The religious sellers had to make sure that their packages were targeted at the right clientele and that their presentation was succinct and compelling enough to catch potential adherents.

Paul's speech on the Areopagus (Acts 17:22–24) shows how he engaged in precisely that kind of competition with the Romans and their gods.

> Paul, standing in the middle of the Areopagus, said, "Athenian men, I perceive that you are religious in every way, for when as I walked along observing your objects of worship, I found also an altar upon which had been inscribed TO AN UNKNOWN GOD. So the one you worship as unknown, I announce to you [openly]. The God who fabricated the world and everything in it, who is Lord of heaven and earth, does not dwell in temples made by hand.

This chapter presents the three strongest competitors to the early Christian message. Two of these religions, Manicheanism and Hermeticism, eventually faded away, though traces of them can be found in surviving religious and esoteric traditions. The third, Neoplatonic philosophy, was so powerful that Christian bishops appropriated many of its philosophical premises and made them the basis for orthodox Christian doctrine.

WHO WERE THE MANICHEANS?

Nowadays, the word "Manichean" is mostly used as a pejorative for someone who understands morality as a strict dualism of good and evil. That popular definition hardly does justice to the subtlety and beauty of the ancient Manichean religion. I will begin my introduction to it with another analogy.

We have all known people who will buy only foods that are fully certified as organic. Some of these people are so zealous that they continually remind the rest of us about the evils of chemical fertilizers, pesticides, genetic alterations, and everything else that is nonorganic. If you listen closely to the most rigid of these "organicophiles" (as I will call them), you would think that your lettuce is dripping with carcinogenic chemicals, that your apples might infect you with pesticides, that your milk has been injected with dangerous bacteria—that anything that you might want to eat should be considered toxic unless it is thoroughly organic. Now these organicophiles may have a point—most of the time I trust their judgment. But from their perspective the world aligns itself into just two camps: the destructive camp of chemically enhanced food items, and the healthful camp of organically grown and produced food items. And never shall the two meet.

That is how the Manicheans understood their world. Yes, it was a world that was starkly divided between the light and the dark, the good and the evil, the right and the wrong, but it was not a world of ill will, for it provided the Manichean with an opportunity to choose the right, to select the good, and to embrace the light. It was an unruly and dangerous world, but the Manicheans knew how to save it.

Mani, the founder of the sect, was born in Persia in 216 C.E. (and died in 276). Persia stood at the crossroads of East and West on what was called the "silk road," the ancient trading route from China to the Mediterranean basin. There was also a brisk trade in religion.

Persia was the home of the ancient religion called Zoroastrianism, another strictly dualistic religion founded by Zoroaster (ca. 630–550 B.C.E.). Though Mani was reared in the Zoroastrian context, he also had early encounters with Christianity and Buddhism, as well as all the other religions whose members traveled and traded along the ancient silk road.

Mani was a visionary. In his youth he had a vision of his heavenly twin, a divine aspect of himself from which he was separated but with whom he still communicated. This vision impelled him to join a sect called the Elkasites, who combined Christian and Jewish teachings and focused on rites of cleansing and transformation through baptism. Mani hoped that the Elkasites would help him reunite with his heavenly twin and become whole.

But Mani's days among the Elkasites were numbered. Soon he received another revelation and began to preach about it. After the Elkasites expelled him in 240 he undertook a mission to India. Upon his return in 242, he used his family connections to gain access to the Persian court and converted many of its members.

WHAT DID THE MANICHEANS BELIEVE?

Mani understood himself to be an "apostle of light," the latest in a long line of significant revealers of the true way: Jesus, Paul, the Christian apostles, Buddha, and the prophets of Israel. Mani himself was the final apostle, the one in whom the entire revelation culminated, the divine Paraclete that Jesus had promised (John 14:15–17), who would lead all people to an understanding of the truth.

And what was that truth? At the dawn of creation, the cosmos had consisted of two mutually exclusive but harmoniously complementary worlds: the world of light and the world of darkness. These worlds coexisted without conflict until the devil decided to invade the world of light so that he could take control of it. The cosmology and the myth get complicated, but what results is simple. The material world came into being as a devourer of the light—a place where it's held captive. The goal of human existence—and the salvation of all created beings— is to return the light to its proper realm. Here is a verse from a Manichean hymn about the captive light:

> Look! The great saving kingdom stands above, ready to receive those who have knowledge so that they may eventually find peace there. [An evil principle] runs brutishly from place to place, giving no peace whatsoever to the upper and lower limbs of Light. She captures and binds the Light in [five] huge bodies: earth, water, fire, plants, and animals. She molds it into different forms; she makes it into many figures; she binds it in prison so that it cannot rise up to the height. She encloses it in a net; she piles it high; she guards it.

This idea would resonate in medieval Jewish Kabbalah more than a thousand years later, as the imperative to "raise the sparks."

How did one know that this process was occurring? In two ways. First, the waxing and waning of the moon. This resulted from the monthly accumulation and eventual release of the light particles into the heavens. If a Manichean watched the cycles of the moon, he would see the result of redemption happening on the earth. Second, the stars themselves pointed the way. The Milky Way was the road the light takes when it travels from the moon back to its source.

Now we have the picture of how it all fit together. But how was this a religion? The theology and the practice of Manicheanism revolved about assisting in the release of the light particles from their material prison. Manicheans achieved this by processing food. (Now you understand why I thought of the analogy of the organic food fanatics.)

The entire physical universe contained elements of light, but some foods held it in particularly high concentrations: especially melons, bread, and water. By eating these foods and digesting them, Manicheans released light particles from their bodies.

Manichean religion was ascetic in that it controlled and manipulated the body in order to achieve a religious goal, the release of light. Fruit and vegetable plants responded most fully to the light, so the Manicheans were strict vegetarians. The killing of animals, for food or any other reason, was strictly forbidden, as violence was understood to perpetuate the realm of darkness and evil. Since the fleshly pleasures of sexual intercourse and the production of children furthered the forces of darkness, the Manicheans were vigorous advocates of sexual abstinence, too. Some Manicheans also seem to have believed in a form of reincarnation. Lesser members of the order—called "hearers" or "auditors"—hoped to be returned to life as vegetables or fruits so they could be eaten and digested and thus aid in the return of light to its proper realm.

The Manichean church (and it was called a "church") was dedicated to this process. The Manicheans differentiated between two primary classes of people: the elect and the hearers. The Manichean elect functioned as light-releasing machines. Forbidden to own property or to support themselves, the elect were itinerant teachers (they also produced elaborate copies of sacred manuscripts). They fasted nearly a hundred days a year, and did no other work but attend to the release of light.

The hearers, on the other hand, were the workers in the organization. Their job was to support and provide for the elect. In return, the elect forgave them for their sins—sins they incurred, of course, by picking fruits and preparing vegetables for the elect to eat. The Manicheans demanded that the hearers, also called the catechumens (or "those who were being instructed"), live a highly moral and upright life. While the elect dealt with the heavenly realm, the hearers lived in the workaday world, where their morality alone distinguished them from those outside the church. Here is an excerpt from a hymn for a hearer's funeral:

> I, a divine form, have been placed in this world, bereft of
> my heavenly clothing. I saw the redeemer. He spoke to
> me gently and lovingly. In my constant subjugation, hope
> returned to me. The wonder enlightened me. My mind

was filled with joy. My life has ended so quickly! Liberate me from the terrible affliction today in my dying!
Come, redeemer; come saving God, Lord Mani. We are
praising you. . . . Gracious God, remember me, an audi-
tor, a trusting soul, your beloved child, an obedient follower. Gracious God, remember me, for my thoughts
focus on the last day. Come, God, look at me. Be my
helper at the time of my death.

The Manicheans prayed four times a day. They practiced
some sort of baptism for entry into the church and held a
form of fulfillment of their duties in a sacred meal, although
scant information about these sacraments has survived. The
Manichean liturgical books—prayers, psalms, homilies, and
lectures—were some of the most beautiful manuscripts in the
ancient world.

Reading was an arduous task in antiquity. In the first place,
books were read aloud, requiring a reader to put on a perfor-
mance. In addition, they were written in continuous script,
without any breaks between the words. Since each line had
enough room for only a certain number of letters, they simply
spilled over from one line to the next, whether a word was
completed or not. Here is an example of continuous script:

> readingwasanarduoustaskinantiquityinthefi
> rstplacebookswerereadaloudrequiringarea

Imagine trying to read hundreds of pages of this and you get
the idea. By making the experience of reading one of their
manuscripts aesthetically pleasing as well as intellectually stim-

ulating, the Manicheans appealed to the intellectuals in a community. While arduously trying to make sense of the letters on the page, the Manicheans gave the reader something else to ponder: beautiful illustrations, vivid colors, rich ornamentation in gold. Reading a Manichean book gave pleasure to all the senses.

The Manicheans considered themselves authentic Christians but obviously the orthodox Christians did not reciprocate. Nonetheless, they established churches and monasteries in North Africa, northern Italy, France, and the Balkans, throughout Egypt, Syria, and Persia, and as far east as Tibet and China. Chinese Manichean texts, found in Chang'an, the capital of the Tang dynasty, were produced between the tenth and the twelfth centuries c.e., attesting to the longevity and popularity of this religion.

The Manicheans' love of beauty, visual and verbal alike, attracted many people to their way of life. Their ability to gather disparate people into categories not of race or culture, but of those who bear the light, allowed them to become a unifying force in an increasingly diverse world.

WHO WERE THE HERMETICISTS?

A good friend once urged me to read a current book on plasma physics and chaos theory by a well-known scientist. The first few chapters weren't easy, but I made the effort and was able to understand them. But as I got deeper into the book and the theories became ever more complex and interrelated, I found myself facing a wall of words that held virtually no meaning for me. Eventually I did finish, I certainly picked up a great deal of information along the way (although I hope I'm never evaluated on what I think I may have learned!), but I know I hardly even scratched the book's surface.

Scientific knowledge constitutes a whole other world for which a person needs initiation and training to even begin to understand the basic concepts. It functions like an esoteric system, closed to those who have not been admitted to its greater mysteries. That helpless sense of standing before a vast universe, needing guidance, direction, and initiation, is precisely the experience that the Hermeticists addressed. The Hermeticists helped people break through the barrier of their limited knowledge, experience the wide complexity of the universe, and contemplate the mysteries of life with confidence and grace.

Hermes Trismegistus, literally Hermes the "three times greatest," is the Greek name for the Egyptian god Thoth, the origin and protector of knowledge in the Egyptian pantheon. The men who organized themselves around the revelations of Hermes Trismegistus valued the intellectual life and the process of guiding younger men in their intellectual development. I say "men," because no evidence exists that the cult of Hermes Trismegistus included women.

They were the best spiritual directors in the ancient world. The Hermeticists understood how to train people to know, to understand, and to grow in their spiritual and intellectual life, and to achieve incredible depths of meditation and prayer. That was no small order.

All of their writings engaged the reader immediately. Here is a paraphrase of the introduction to the Hermetic treatise *Poimandres*, which means "The Shepherd":

I was hanging around once, and it occurred to me to think about life and I tried to think about the great issues of living. But my body kept me back. It seemed to lull me to sleep, to weigh me down, when suddenly a huge being appeared to me and said, "So what is it that you want to hear and see? What do you want to learn and to know?" So I asked him, "Who are you?" And he answered, "I am the Shepherd, the ruling mind. I know what you seek, and I am always with you." So I said to him, "I am desperately eager to learn about existence and to know god."

The Shepherd gives the young man a vision and then explains, through dialogue, the meaning of the ultimate questions of the young man's life. All of the Hermetic literature had this quality of restless intellectual seeking—it joined theological and philosophical speculations with science, astrology, anthropology, and every other kind of knowledge. Hermeticists were eager to explore it all. The following Hermetic prayer of thanksgiving provides an eloquent illustration of their thirst for *gnosis:*

We thank you! Every mind and heart lifts up to you, O Name that cannot be troubled, dignified with the name "God" and glorified with the name "Father," for you bestow upon every person and every thing your paternal kindness and affection and love. You bestow also every sweet and clear teaching, giving us mind, speech, and knowledge: mind to understand you; speech to explain you; knowledge to know you. Having been illumined by your knowledge, we rejoice. We rejoice also because you have revealed yourself to us. We rejoice because even while still embodied, you

*divinized us through your knowledge. For those who have as-
cended to you there is only one thing worthy of thanks: our
knowledge of you. We know you, cerebral light. We know you, life
of life. We know you, womb birthing every creature. We know
you, womb pregnant with the Father's reality. So we worship
your goodness, eternal duration of the Father who generates. We
ask only one thing: preserve us in this knowledge. We ask for only
one security: let us not stumble in this way of life.*

—THE DISCOURSE ON THE EIGHTH AND NINTH,

NHL VI, 63,33–65,7

This knowledge had a theological purpose—it was intended
to save people. Knowledge brought the initiates into deeper
and deeper contemplation. Knowledge enabled the Hermeticists not simply to know God, but to experience God directly.
The elder members of the Hermetic cult helped the younger
ones to move forward not only in their minds, but in their spir-
its and bodies as well.

The Nag Hammadi treatise *The Discourse on the Eighth and
Ninth* provides precious insights into the process of spiritual
direction. We do not often have access to such information
from the ancient world, so this is quite unusual. First the initiate was told to remember all the steps of learning he had been
taught, and to recall all the knowledge he had found in the
books he had been told to read. Since this instruction and reading connected the initiate to the other seekers in his spiritual
community, he was instructed to bring the spiritual brother-
hood to mind as well. The spiritual guide connected the initiate to the source of all wisdom. He was the well, the spring, the

source of that experience. This preparatory step concluded with prayer.

The second step began with a brief liturgy of embrace that empowered the guide to lead the initiate. The guide said, "Let us embrace affectionately, my son." The embrace transformed the guide, who announced, "I am mind and I see the other mind that moves the soul" and "You give me power! I see myself! I want to speak." The guide now had taken on the persona of Hermes Trismegistus.

This second step ended with a silent hymn. The guide told the initiate, "Sing, for I am Mind." The initiate responded: "I name you father, the *Aeon* of the *Aeons,* the great divine spirit. And by a spirit he gives rain upon everyone. What do you say to me, O my father Hermes?" The complete identification of the guide with Hermes allowed the initiate to experience the god directly and immediately in his interaction with his guide.

In the third step the initiate received a vision of the end of the heavenly spheres, where he would pass from the material world completely into the spiritual: "I see the eighth with the souls that are in it and the angels making hymns to the ninth and its powers. And I see him who has the power of them all, who creates those who are in the spirit." This vision completed the initiation, and ended with this amazing hymn:

> I will sing the praise that is in my mind, as I pray to the
> end of the universe, and to the beginning of the begin-
> ning, the human's quest, the immortal discovery, the
> begetter of light and truth, the sower of the discourse, the
> love of immortal life. No hidden discourse will be able to

speak concerning you, Lord. Therefore my mind desires
to make hymns to you daily. I am the organ of your spirit;
the mind is your plectrum; and your counsel plucks me. I
see myself. I have received power from you, for your love
has touched us.

The experience was almost complete. The initiate had become
an adept, a master, now capable of guiding others in the search
for knowledge and the experience of the divine.

There was one last step, however: the writing of a book. The
guide instructed the newly initiated: "O my son, write this
book in hieroglyphic characters for the Diospolis temple." The
process ended with the continuation of knowledge and learning, in books that articulated the engagement with God and
thus helped others to find the way.

THE LEGACY OF THE HERMETICISTS

The Hermeticists' ability to create intense and loving communities of spiritually alive, intellectually expansive, and socially
responsible seekers posed a serious challenge to Christianity.
There was no room here for blind faith or mindless trust, such
as the Christian bishops demanded from their faithful. Soon
some Christian churches would require their baptizands to un-
dergo a similar initiation of reading and study, so that by the
time of their baptism they would be completely transformed—
an idea taken almost directly from their Hermeticist rivals.

In 1462 Cosimo de' Medici commissioned Marcilio Ficino,
the famous Italian scholar and authority on ancient languages,

to translate into Latin the Greek text of the Hermetic treatises, which he had just secured from the Byzantine East for a Florentine library. This began a craze for Hermetic literature that has not abated to this day. For the Renaissance intellectuals the Hermetic literature represented a philosophical and theological system uncontaminated by Christian orthodoxy and hence not tired and dull, but alive and satisfying. Hermeticism would continue to play a large role in alchemy and a variety of other occult and esoteric movements, such as Rosicrucianism and theosophy, and is a major influence on the contemporary New Age movement.

WHAT IS NEOPLATONISM?

Wisdom leads the soul to the place of God. There is no kinsman of the truth except wisdom. It is not possible for a believing nature to become fond of lying. A fearful and slavish nature will not be able to partake in faith.

—*SENTENCES OF SEXTUS*, SAYINGS 167–170, NHLE

Entering the world of the Neoplatonists is like walking into the main reading room of the Library of Congress. Its spectacular ceilings and beautiful adornments awe you; its proportions make you feel small and important all at once. Everything has its place. Every book is in order, waiting for you to call it forth from the library stacks. Every person stands ready to take your direction. The lighting is perfect; spacious reading tables and comfortable chairs await you. The whole room feels as though it is waiting for you to begin your study. This is how the Neoplatonists experienced the divine cosmos—as well ordered, perfectly balanced, eager and ready for the seeker to engage mind and soul in its study.

The Neoplatonist school of philosophy began with the philosopher Plotinus (205–270 C.E.). Plotinus and his successors founded their system on the philosophy of the Academy, the Platonist school that continued to function in Athens from the time of Plato (427–347 B.C.E.) until Justinian closed it in 529 C.E. Porphyry (232–305 C.E.) was Plotinus's student and an editor of his philosophical writing; he also wrote a biography, *Life and Works*, which provides fascinating insights into Plotinus's life and character. Here are a few exemplary passages:

> When it came to his writing, he could not bear to revise his prose twice. He could also not bear to read through things twice because his eyesight was too poor for reading. So he wrote, not with a lovely handwriting and barely separating the syllables or attending to proper spelling. [When he wrote] he was all mind. This amazed us. He would work things through in his mind until they were complete. So he would complete the topic for analysis completely in his mind from start to finish, then he would write it down. And when he wrote, he created it such that it seemed he was transcribing something that was completely formulated in his mind as though he were copying it from a book. Even when someone interrupted him to have a conversation, he continued his own thought processes in his mind so that at one and the same time he conversed and worked out a philosophical problem without any interruption in either process. When his conver-

sation partner left . . . he simply picked up where he was writing as though he were not interrupted at all. So he could attend to himself and to others at the same time. And he never broke his concentration except to sleep, which he warded off with eating only a little food (he never ate bread!) and his continual turning of his effort toward things of the mind.

Women also became his devoted students. Gemina, in whose house he lived, and her daughter Gemina, named for her mother, and Amphiclea . . . all devoted themselves to philosophy.

Many noble men and women, knowing that they were going to die soon, brought their male and female children, to give them to him with all their earthly belongings as to a kind of holy and devout keeper. So his house was always filled with children. . . . Yet so long as he was awake, he never disturbed the intensity of his thinking. This even while he was overseeing the life and concerns of so many in his household. He was always gracious and receptive to anyone who sought him out. Having lived in Rome for twenty-six years, often mediating between disputants, he never made a political enemy.

He was a superior judge of character. Once someone stole an expensive necklace from Chione, who lived out her noble widowhood living together with her children in his household. So he gathered all the household into one place, and looking at all of them announced, "This is the thief," pointing to a particular person. That person denied

it, even though he was whipped severely. Later, however,
he confessed and returned the necklace.

Christian theologians would adapt Neoplatonic thought as
they developed the major doctrines of the church: the theology
of the incarnation, the way in which Jesus displayed both humanity and divinity in one person; the doctrine of the Trinity,
the relationship of the three persons (Father, Son, and Holy
Spirit) and their common divine substance; and the central role
of contemplation both to theology and to the practice of Christian religion.

But in 361, when Julian (332–363 C.E.), the half brother of
Constantine, became emperor, Neoplatonism became more
than an influence on Christianity—it threatened to supplant it
altogether. Although he was raised as a Christian, Julian renounced his Christianity and attempted to reinstate Roman
philosophical religion and sacrifice as the imperial religion.
Christians called him the "apostate."

A prolific writer, Julian studied philosophy at the Academy
in Athens in 355. He composed hymns in honor of the gods
and another hymn in honor of the mother of the gods, and he
wrote books attacking Christianity. Here is some of the advice
he gave to his Roman priesthood—advice that is generally im-
itative of the Christian priesthood of his day:

> We really should share our money with everyone, and
> even more generously with the helpless and poverty-
> stricken in order to make up their need. It might sound
> somewhat strange to say, I also think it would be really a

fine and pious act to share our clothes and food with evil people, because we give not to a particular characteristic but to the basic humanity of the person. I even think prisoners deserve the same sort of consideration because this kind of philanthropy enhances justice. . . .

I propose that everyone base their manner of life on the ethical virtues and performances such as veneration for the gods, benefaction toward other people, personal continence. Then let everyone perform many pious deeds, specifically by attempting always to consider the gods in a pious way, and by honoring the sanctuaries and images of the gods with great respect and adoration, and by worshipping the gods as though they were standing right before you.

The "philosophical religion" that Julian imposed on the empire was Neoplatonism. Julian considered it a perfect substitute for Christianity, and he systematically dismantled the imperial privilege Christians had enjoyed since Constantine. His efforts came to an end when he was killed on the battlefield in Persia in 363.

WHAT DID THE NEOPLATONISTS BELIEVE?

The Neoplatonists asked a very simple and yet compelling question: How can all beings come from one common source when they differ so much from each other? They asked this question of the one and the many, the common and the diverse.

And they gave a compelling answer in the form of a cosmic story.

The Neoplatonists imagined a primal unity that was the origin of all beings. This was the One, an unknowable source of all goodness, beauty, existence, and life. From the superabundance of its goodness and goodwill, the One overflowed and descended to establish the next spiritual level of existence, the *Nous*, which means intelligence and intuitive knowledge. The *Nous*, imitating and following the way established by the One, also overflowed from the abundance of its intellect to create the next lower spiritual level of the universe, the Soul. The Soul was the cosmic mind of the universe. It constituted the ideal form of all created things—in a way, it was the spiritual DNA of the created universe. Just as the One and the *Nous* had, the Soul also overflowed with its own goodness and rationality, and the created universe emerged.

The Universe, or Nature, consisted of all existent beings—starting from the most ethereal and spiritual, the astrological spheres of the universe, down to the most physical, things such as rocks and dirt. The Universe itself, in this way, imitated the action of the One, the *Nous*, and the Soul to spill over into creation. As the downward flow of creation moved away from the spiritual and toward the purely physical, it became a ladder of beings, devolving ever more into things farthest from the One. That distance from the One, manifest in degrees of materiality, defined what is evil, or bad, or nonexistent.

What an amazing image of the cosmos! Everything ultimately was held together as a phenomenon or thing emanating from the One, and yet everything differed from the One and had its own proper existence and being. Diversity and unity cohered. The Neoplatonic system also cohered by participation. As it emanated from the One, each lower level continued to have its root in the One and to participate in the life and being of the One. The flow held all things in a common unity, while the levels at which various beings existed differentiated them. Humans participated in the One by following upward the path of the emanation to become ever higher and more spiritual beings—up through the Soul, through the *Nous,* and ultimately to the One. And the same held true in reverse. The One descended to humans through the *Nous,* the Soul, and the spiritual elements of the created universe.

This great chain of being was a dynamic process of emanation and return. Life flowed downward from the One to the most material substance in creation, and love flowed upward back to the One. The created world trembled with the energy of simultaneous movement in both directions.

Human beings stood at the very center of the Universe: above them were purely spiritual beings without material bodies; below them were beings with gradually decreasing souls, until they were purely material. Simultaneously estranged from the One and yearning for the One, the human condition was defined by distance and longing. The restoration and salvation of the human, the fulfillment of all human desire, began by gradually ascending the ladder of being until the human achieved union with the One.

This was achieved by contemplation, a gradual process of upward movement from the embodied state. That process began with a period of preparation, a cleansing of the mind and body, a gradual withdrawal from the concerns of bodily living until the mind was filled only with spiritual and intellectual concerns. Leaving the bodily behind, the mind started its ascent—first in contemplation of the spiritual universe, then to Soul, then *Nous,* eventually to a mental union with the One, a kind of ecstatic and mystical union of the mind with the One. Later, Byzantine and medieval Christians adopted this contemplative practice without much alteration. It would become the bedrock of Christian mystical and spiritual transformation.

THE LEGACY OF NEOPLATONISM

Part of the reason that Neoplatonism was so congenial to early—and later—Christians was that Neoplatonists also valued revelation as the basis of their understanding and knowledge. The Neoplatonists sought these revelations in philosophical texts and oracles, and in treatises on magic and alchemy (the "science" of turning base physical elements into gold) and used them to supplement their system.

Christian revelations largely resided in the holy scriptures of the Old and New Testaments. These could be read as oracular texts that revealed the unity of all things in the One True God. The story of Genesis 1 and 2, about the creation of the world, for example, could be elucidated as a story of the emanation of the divine love overflowing into the created universe. There is no inconsistency here. Christianity became in the end a theological child of Neoplatonism—most of the early theologians who framed the doctrinal basis for orthodox Christianity, especially regarding the incarnation, the Trinity, and the contemplative life, were influenced by this philosophy.

The Cappadocian fathers were three early Christian theologians from the province of Cappadocia (in modern Turkey): Basil of Caesarea (330–379), Gregory of Nyssa (330–395), and Gregory of Nanzianzus (330–390). They developed theological explanations of the Christian Trinity, the relationship of the Father to the Son and to the Holy Spirit, and the two natures of Christ (both human and divine). Basil and Gregory of Nanzianzus both studied at the Academy in Athens. Their articulation of the way the human and divine natures of Christ coexisted in one person, and of the manner in which the emanation of Son from Father, and Spirit from Father, could take place before the creation of the world, is thoroughly informed by Neoplatonic philosophy.

We began this book with an account of the Nicene Council, where, among other things, the bishops debated the Arian heresy, which stated that Jesus came into being in time as the first element in the creation of the world. If this sounds philosophical, it is. The orthodox of Nicaea affirmed that the Son was generated within the divine person before the creation, while the Arians seem to have thought "there was a time when the Son was not," that is, that the Son was part of the Father's creative process. The word used by the orthodox bishops to describe Jesus' status vis-à-vis the Father was *homoousios*, "being of the same essence," as opposed to *homoiousios*, "being of similar essence." The distinction may be a subtle one, but to the Neoplatonically trained bishops it was immensely important. The first, "being of the same essence," identified the Son with the primordial divine essence that created all beings. The second, "being of similar essence," created a kind of gulf between the primordial divine essence and the Son, leaving room for the notion that the Son was a lesser being. It is virtually impossible to understand the Nicene Creed without first understanding the philosophy of late antiquity. They are completely fused and interrelated.

APPENDIX 1

The following is the full text of Clement's letter to Theodore:

From among the letters of Clement [of Alexandria] of the Stromateis [fame].

To Theodore:

You did well to curb the shameful teachings of the Carpocratians. For these are the ones prophesied to be the "roaming stars," who roam away from the laws [of God] into an unbounded abyss of fleshly and bodily sins. For, since they are puffed up in knowledge, as they say, "of the deep things of Satan," they forget that they throw themselves into the "nether darkness" of false doctrine. And since they boast that they are free [of restraints], they have become slaves of abject desires. One must oppose such as these [heretics] in every way and at all times. For even if they were to say something true, the lover of truth ought not to agree with them even then. For not all true things are truth. Neither should one prefer the truth that appears [to be] true according to human opinions over the true truth according to the faith.

Now concerning the things they chatter about the divinely inspired gospel of Mark, some are completely false and others are not transmitted truly even if [the writing] contains some true [statements]. The true things being blended with the counterfeit will be debased such that, as is clear in the saying, "salt becomes insipid."

Mark, then, wrote up the Lord's acts according to Peter's teaching in Rome. He did not make known all [his acts], nor did he throw out hints about secret [ones]. He rather chose what he considered most useful for the faith of the catechumens. But when Peter was martyred, Mark came to Alexandria carrying away both his own and Peter's notes so as to preserve them. From among these notes he transferred to his first book the things appropriate to [those who wish to make] progress concerning knowledge (*gnosis*). He composed a more spiritual gospel for the use of those who were [advancing toward] perfection. In no way did he let out the things shameful to say; nor did he write down the mystical teaching of the Lord. Rather, to the acts already written he added other [acts], and besides he brought forth certain sayings [of the Lord], whose interpretation he believed will initiate the hearers into the innermost sanctuary of the seven-veiled truth. In this way he prepared [the book] neither begrudgingly nor unguardedly, in my opinion. And when he died he left the same writing to the church in Alexandria where it is to this time carefully guarded, being read only to those who are being initiated into the greater mysteries.

Since the polluted demons always contrive destruction for the human race, Carpocrates, taught by them and employing [their] deceptive arts, so enslaved a presbyter of the church of Alexandria that he procured from him a copy of the mystical gospel. He explained it according to his blasphemous and fleshly opinion, and even more he polluted the pure and holy words by mixing them with his most shameful lies. The doctrine of Carpocrates is drawn from this mixture.

One must never yield to them, as I said earlier. One must not concede that the gospel is Mark's when they bring forth their falsifications, but one must deny it with an oath, because one must not speak every truth to everyone. This is why the Wisdom of God announced through Solomon: "Answer the fool with his foolishness," [thereby] teaching that the light of the truth should be hidden from the intellectually blind. [Wisdom] also says, "It shall be taken away from the one who has," and "Let the fool walk in darkness." But we are "children of light" who have been enlightened by "the dayspring from on high" of the spirit of the Lord. And it says, "Where the Spirit of the Lord is, there is freedom," for "all things are pure to the pure."

So, I will not hesitate to answer your questions by exposing the falsifications by [quoting] the words of the gospel. For instance, after "And they were on the road going up to Jerusalem," and what follows until "After three days he will arise," here [the mystical gospel] brings forth [and I quote it] word for word:

> And they came to Bethany and there was there a woman whose brother had died. And coming forward she fell down and worshipped Jesus and said to him, "Son of David, have mercy on me," but the disciples rebuked her. And Jesus, becoming angry, went with her into the garden where the tomb was. And immediately a great voice was heard from within the tomb. Jesus approached and rolled away the stone from the door of the tomb. Immediately he entered where the young boy was, he stretched out his hand and raised him [from the dead], holding on to his hand. And the young boy, looking upon him, loved him, and he began to entreat him that he might be with him. And exiting the tomb, they came to the house of the young boy, for he was wealthy. After six days, Jesus ordered him. When it was evening, the young boy comes to him wearing a linen cloth over

his naked body. And he remained with him that night, for Jesus taught him the mystery of the Kingdom of God. From there, arising, he went to the other side of the Jordan.

And after these words follow [these words]: "And James and John attended him" and all the [rest of] the section. But the phrase "naked man with naked man" about which you wrote is not found.

And after [the words] "And he comes into Jericho," follows [in the mystical gospel] only [the words]: "And the sister of the young boy whom Jesus loved and his mother and Salome were there, and Jesus did not receive them." And the many other things about which you wrote seem also to be falsifications. Now the true explanation even according to the true philosophy . . . [the text breaks off here].

THE BIBLICAL CANON

One of Marcion's lasting effects on the orthodox church was to spur the development of a biblical canon, an official listing of the authorized and approved texts included in the New Testament. However, the canon remained fluid for some time—although a consensus began to be formed during the second century C.E., it wasn't until the Counter-Reformation of the sixteenth century that the canon was fixed once and for all. Compare some of the following lists of canonical books.

Marcion's canon of the New Testament is as follows:

> The Gospel of Luke
>
> Galatians
>
> 1 Corinthians
>
> 2 Corinthians
>
> Romans
>
> 1 Thessalonians
>
> 2 Thessalonians
>
> Ephesians (called *Laodiceans* by Marcion)
>
> Colossians

Philemon

Philippians

Irenaeus of Lyon, the famous heresy hunter, included only the following short list of books in his version of the New Testament, but note that he included the *Shepherd of Hermas,* a second-century treatise that presents various visions, and omitted many more familiar texts:

>Gospels: Matthew, Mark, Luke, and John
>
>Acts
>
>Pauline Epistles: Romans, 1 and 2 Corinthians, Galatians, Ephesians, Philippians, 1 and 2 Thessalonians, 1 and 2 Timothy, Titus
>
>1 Peter
>
>1 John
>
>Revelation
>
>*The Shepherd of Hermas*

In the second century Clement of Alexandria added these now unfamiliar texts to his canon:

>The *Didache* ("The Teaching of the Twelve Apostles")
>
>*The Apocalypse of Peter*
>
>*The Shepherd of Hermas*
>
>*The Epistle of Barnabas*
>
>*1 Clement*
>
>*The Preaching of Peter*
>
>*The Tradition of Matthias*
>
>*The Gospel of the Hebrews*
>
>*The Gospel of the Egyptians*

The *Didache* was a manual of liturgical, moral, and ethical practices. The *Epistle of Barnabas* was a polemic against Jewish practices; *Clement* was a letter written to the Pauline congregation in Corinth by the bishop of Rome in the late first century. *The Preaching of Peter* was written in the early second century C.E.; it is a pseudepigraphical (i.e., purportedly written in the voice of a biblical character) letter of the apostle Peter. *The Tradition of Matthias* has been attested to only by Clement; only fragments remain of the gospels of the Hebrews and Egyptians.

Eusebius (260–340 C.E.), the first historian of the Christian church, listed the books of the New Testament under four headings: authorized, disputed, spurious, and heretical texts.

Authorized:

> Gospels: Matthew, Mark, Luke, and John
>
> Acts
>
> Pauline Epistles: Romans, 1 and 2 Corinthians, Gala-
> tians, Ephesians, Philippians, 1 and 2 Thessalonians,
> 1 and 2 Timothy, Titus, Philemon, Hebrews
>
> 1 John
>
> 1 Peter

Disputed:

> James
>
> Jude
>
> 2 Peter
>
> 2 and 3 John

Spurious:

> *The Acts of Paul*
>
> *The Shepherd of Hermas*
>
> *The Apocalypse of Peter*
>
> *The Epistle of Barnabas*
>
> *The Gospel of the Hebrews*

The *Didache* ("The Teaching of the Twelve Apostles")
Revelation

Heretical:
> *The Gospel of Peter*
> *The Gospel of Thomas*
> *The Gospel of Matthias*
> *The Acts of Andrew*
> *The Acts of John*

The *Codex Siniaticus* (fourth century C.E.), one of the earliest published complete Bibles, included both the Old and New Testaments and was authorized by the emperor Constantine. In addition to the canonical texts below, it included these two (both of which were considered spurious by Eusebius):

> *The Epistle of Barnabas*
> *The Shepherd of Hermas*

The current canon of the New Testament includes the following:
> Gospels:
> > Matthew
> > Mark
> > Luke
> > John
> > Acts of the Apostles

> Pauline Letters (Authentic):
> > 1 and 2 Thessalonians
> > 1 and 2 Corinthians
> > Philemon

Galatians

Philippians

Romans

Early Pauline School:

Colossians

Ephesians

Hebrews

Pastoral Epistles:

1 and 2 Timothy

Titus

Catholic Epistles:

1 and 2 Peter

James

1, 2, and 3 Letters of John

Jude

Revelation

GLOSSARY

Aeon: A divine being, emanating from God, that became a concrete, cosmic element in the created universe.

archon **(Greek for "ruler"):** One of the divine leaders of the *Aeons* that inhabited the physical and planetary universe.

Arianism: The heresy that maintained that Jesus was part of the created universe (its slogan was "there was a time when he was not"). It was propagated by Arius (ca. 250–336 C.E.), a presbyter of the church in Alexandria, Egypt, and condemned by the first ecumenical council at Nicaea in 324 C.E.

boskoi **(Greek for "grazers" or "shepherds"):** Ascetics in Syria and Asia Minor who roamed the countryside naked, eating like animals on all four limbs, in order to reestablish on earth the Edenic paradise.

Carpocratians: A Gnostic sect founded by Carpocrates that advocated experiencing everything possible in human life, including illicit sexuality, and that revised the spiritual edition of the Gospel of Mark to advance their own particular theology.

catechesis: A course of study for those preparing for baptism.

catechumen: A person enrolled in catechetical instruction for baptism.

cenobitic (from the Greek word for common life): The kind of monastic life in which the monks live together in households, sharing the responsibility for the maintenance of their daily needs and the common life of communal prayer.

Circumcellions: A North African group of radical separatist Christians affiliated with the Donatists who terrorized their religious opponents.

Clement of Alexandria: A famous teacher at the first major Christian institution of higher learning in Alexandria (ca. 150–215), who preserved many fragments of otherwise unknown gospels.

demiurge: The creator of the physical universe, so named by Platonists, Gnostics, and other philosophical and religious movements in antiquity.

Donatist: A heretical movement in North Africa that advocated a strictly pure state for Christians and their clergy; they were condemned by the emperor Constantine.

emanation: A concept in Neoplatonic and Gnostic thought that described the manner in which one level of existence overflowed into the succeeding lower and more physical levels of creation, extending downward from the most spiritual to the most physical.

Encratite (from the Greek word for "continence" or "self-control"): A movement of ascetic Christians who rejected sexuality and marriage in favor of a purely continent and single lifestyle.

eremite (from the Greek word for "desert"): An ascetic monk who lives alone and in isolation (as though in the desert) under the general supervision of a charismatic spiritual guide.

Eusebius of Caesarea: The first church historian (b. ca. 260; d. before 341); he wrote during the reign of the first Christian emperor, Constantine, and preserved many of the earliest documents illustrative of early Christian communities.

exegesis: Interpretation of a passage of scripture, usually accomplished through careful and rigorous textual and theological analysis.

gnosis: Knowledge or understanding, which formed the opposite pole to faith in the early church and characterized the often-secret knowledge of the Gnostics.

Gnostic: One seeking or using secret knowledge in order to achieve salvation.

Gnosticism: A nineteenth-century term used to designate the associations, beliefs, and practices of various Gnostic groups.

heresiologist: A person who studies heresies, especially doctrines and practices that appear to conflict with orthodox theology or to challenge dominant Christian thought.

heresy: A belief considered at odds with the prevailing orthodox theological perspective, which often in the early church was declared heretical by a council of bishops.

homoiousios **(from the Greek meaning "of similar substance"):** The doctrine of the Arians, who maintained that Jesus was the firstborn of the Father in primordial time and therefore was chronologically subsequent to the Father, making him only similar to the Father.

homoousios **(from the Greek meaning "of the same substance"):** The doctrine of the relationship of Jesus to God the Father that maintains that they were of the same divine substance so that Jesus was considered fully divine when he took on the flesh of human identity.

hylic **(from the Greek word meaning "material matter"):** In Gnosticism the kind of person who was merely material and incapable of understanding anything spiritual, in contrast to psychics and pneumatics.

Irenaeus of Lyon: An early bishop of Lyon (ca. 130–202) who wrote a compendium of heresies.

Mani: A prophet who founded a religion intended to liberate the light particles from their bondage in physical matter.

Manicheanism: A religious movement founded by Mani consisting of both leaders and followers, whose duty it was to release the particles of light from their bondage in physical matter.

Marcion: An early intellectual reformer of the Christian church (ca. 85–160 C.E.), who clearly differentiated between the God of the Old Testament, whom he believed to be vengeful and inconsistent, and the God of Jesus Christ, whom he believed was loving and consistent.

Montanus: The founder of a prophetic and apocalyptic movement, which had women prophets (Maximilla and Prisca) and awaited the end of time in Pepuza (modern Turkey). He began preaching around 170 C.E.; his birth and death dates are not known.

Nag Hammadi: A city in Upper Egypt and the site of an early Christian monastery, where the Coptic Gnostic texts, such as the *Gospel of Thomas* and the *Gospel of Philip*, were found.

Neoplatonism: A philosophical movement popular in antiquity that accounted for the created universe through emanation and that provided Christian theologians with a system to explain Christian doctrines.

Nous **(Greek for "mind"):** The highest part of the human person—the other parts are the soul (*psyche*) and the body (*soma*)—which connects the person with God; a kind of intuitive knowledge.

Paraclete **(Greek for "comforter"):** A name for the Christian Holy Spirit, which was believed to be sent by Jesus in the end-time to comfort and lead the church.

pleroma **(Greek for "fullness"):** In Gnosticism the divine fullness in which God dwells together with all the other divine emanations.

pneumatic **(Greek for "spiritual"):** In Gnosticism, a term designating the status of the Gnostic as a spiritual person capable of extraordinary spiritual perception and power in contradistinction to the psychics and the hylics.

psychic (**Greek for "soulful"**): In Gnosticism, a term designating the status of the person who knew of spiritual realities but was unable to pursue them or to perceive their depth, in contrast to hylics and pneumatics.

Sethians: Gnostics who believed that they were the seed of Seth, the spiritual son of Adam, who was to redeem God's people and all creation.

soteriology: A system of salvation, often based on the understanding of a specific salvation figure such as Jesus or Seth.

Stylites: Monks who spent their time atop a pillar in order to be suspended between heaven and earth and so that they could mediate between the things of God and the people on earth.

Valentinians: Adherents of a Gnostic movement founded by Valentinus (ca. 100–175 C.E.), oriented toward plumbing the depths of Christian theology and scripture and committed to remaining within the mainstream Christian church.

The spectacle of early Christian diversity has never ceased to amaze me, even though I have spent most of my life studying it. Its breadth and variety are astonishing: Syrian monks living on top of pillars, Encratites rejecting marriage to keep their bodies pure, Manicheans using their bodily functions to release the light, Gnostics and Hermeticists plotting out the astrological as a guide to salvation, proto-feminist prophets proclaiming a new age. An astonishing array of Christianities, all of them vanished.

The study of vanished Christianities should spur our thinking about religion today, which is no less diverse than it was in the ancient world. The great world religions compete and conflict with each other; Christianity's many denominations are continually arguing about who possesses "the truth." We even have revivals of those ancient churches—Gnostics, followers of the *Gospel of Thomas,* New Age spirituality. Diversity, and the violence it seems to bring in its wake, marks our world as much as it did the ancients'. But does it have to be so? Does anyone possess the full truth? Can anyone speak God's mind definitively?

I hope you find these questions as fascinating as I do and that reading this book has spurred your curiosity about the strange and wonderful beliefs of early Christianity. If you're interested in exploring further, here are some resources that will help to guide you on your way.

GENERAL REFERENCE

It is easier now than in the past to get many of the texts that I refer to in this book by simply searching the Web. For copyright reasons the translations found on the Web are often very old-fashioned, often dating from the nineteenth century. But they are there. I suggest http://earlychristianwritings.com as a good place to begin exploring. For New Testament literature, http://ntgateway.com provides access to a wide assortment of texts, translations, and commentaries.

The *Catholic Encyclopedia* (both in print and online) provides brief and trustworthy articles on the various subjects covered in this book. The *Oxford Dictionary of the Christian Church* (second edition) is a concise, all-purpose reference guide with excellent bibliographies and suggestions for further reading.

EARLY CHRISTIAN LITERATURE—COLLECTIONS OF TEXTS

For a convenient collection of all the gospel materials (including Mark, Matthew, Luke, John, Mary, and Thomas) check out *The Complete Gospels,* edited by Robert Miller. Miller uses the Scholars Version, a contemporary and very accessible translation of the texts.

For the ancient Christian novels, and much more New Testament apocryphal literature, the best collection remains *New Testament Apocrypha*, edited by Wilhelm Schneemelcher (revised edition in two volumes, Westminster/John Knox Press, 1992). The first volume covers the gospels; the second covers writings attributed to the apostles. The translators have provided comprehensive introductions to each of the texts.

For a collection of texts from across the spectrum of religious expression from the second through the seventh centuries, see my own *Religions of Late Antiquity in Practice*. Here you'll find Manichean, Gnostic, Neoplatonist, and Christian texts from Syria, Egypt, Rome, Asia Minor, and Greece, as well as ancient Persia (modern Iraq and Iran). The translators have written accessible introductions to the texts and offer excellent suggestions for further reading.

THE HISTORICAL JESUS

The Jesus Seminar has produced controversial and challenging research about Jesus and his mission. I recommend the works of three members of the Seminar in particular. John Dominic Crossan's *Jesus: A Revolutionary Biography* presents Jesus as a poor, itinerant revolutionary, while Marcus Borg's *Meeting Jesus Again for the First Time* provides fresh new insights into the historical Jesus and his significance for today. Stephen J. Patterson's *The God of Jesus* commends the work of the Jesus Seminar to clergy who are eager to integrate its insights into their parish life.

Much of the research into the historical Jesus depends upon a close examination of the sayings that can be attributed to him with the highest degree of confidence. A critical edition of Q, the sayings collection used by Matthew and Mark in the composition of their gospels, has just been published by James M. Robinson, Paul Hoffmann, and John S. Kloppenborg (*The Say-*

ings Gospel Q in Greek and English, Fortress Press, 2002). My own *The New Q: Translation and Commentary* provides fresh translations and interpretations. The *Gospel of Thomas* is a rich resource for studying Jesus; see my *Gospel of Thomas.*

OVERVIEWS OF RELIGIOUS THOUGHT AND PRACTICE

Of course, no one could take up these subjects without mentioning the popular books that have stirred up such interest in these vanished Christianities. Elaine Pagels's *The Gnostic Gospels* put Gnostic Christianity on the public agenda, while Bart Ehrman's *Lost Christianities* has fanned the flames of interest in these fascinating expressions of Christian life and identity. Pagels's *Beyond Belief* continues the tradition of exploring alternative Christianities for the general reader.

For readers who are willing to tackle less accessible, more academic texts, Margaret R. Miles's *Word Made Flesh* studies theological texts in the context of both art and music. Peter Brown's *The World of Late Antiquity* presents an overview of the history and culture of ancient Christianity in its Roman context. Both of these superb books are filled with valuable information and resources for further study.

RECOMMENDED READINGS

Attridge, Harold, Robert Hodgson Jr., and Charles Hedrick (eds.),
   Nag Hammadi, Gnosticism, and Early Christianity (Peabody, MA:
   Hendrickson Publishers, 1986).
Barnstone, Willis, and Marvin Meyer (eds.), *The Gnostic Bible: Gnostic
   Texts of Mystical Wisdom from the Ancient and Medieval Worlds*
   (Boston: Shambhala, 2003).

Bauer, Walter, *Orthodoxy and Heresy in Earliest Christianity* (Mifflintown, PA: Sigler Press, 1996 reprint).

Borg, Marcus, *The Heart of Christianity: Rediscovering a Life of Faith* (San Francisco: HarperSanFrancisco, 2004).

——. *Meeting Jesus Again for the First Time: The Historical Jesus and the Heart of Contemporary Faith* (San Francisco: HarperSanFrancisco, 1995).

Brown, Peter R. L., *The Rise of Western Christendom: Triumph and Diversity, A.D. 200–1000* (Oxford: Blackwell, 2003).

——. *The World of Late Antiquity A.D. 150–750* (New York: W. W. Norton, 1989).

Crossan, John Dominic, *Jesus: A Revolutionary Biography* (San Francisco: HarperSanFrancisco, 1995).

Ehrman, Bart, *Lost Christianities: The Battle for Scripture and the Faiths We Never Knew* (Oxford: Oxford University Press, 2003).

——. *Lost Scriptures: Books That Did Not Make It into the New Testament* (Oxford: Oxford University Press, 2003).

Jensen, Robin Margaret, *Face to Face: Portraits of the Divine in Early Christianity* (Minneapolis: Fortress Press, 2005).

Jonas, Hans, *The Gnostic Religion* (Boston: Beacon Press, 2001 reprint).

King, Karen, *The Gospel of Mary of Magdala: Jesus and the First Woman Apostle* (Santa Rosa, CA: Polebridge Press, 2003).

——. *What Is Gnosticism?* (Cambridge, MA: Harvard University Press, 2003).

Lampe, Peter, *Christians at Rome in the First Two Centuries* (Minneapolis: Fortress Press, 2003).

Layton, Bentley, *The Gnostic Scriptures: A New Translation with Annotations and Introductions* (New York: Anchor Bible, 1995).

Meyer, Marvin, *The Gospel of Thomas: The Hidden Sayings of Jesus* (San Francisco: HarperSanFrancisco, 1982).

———. *The Gospels of Mary: The Secret Tradition of Mary Magdalene, the Companion of Jesus* (San Francisco: HarperSanFrancisco, 2004).

———. *The Secret Teachings of Jesus: Four Gnostic Gospels* (New York: Vintage Books, 1986).

Miles, Margaret R., *Image as Insight: Visual Understanding in Western Christianity and Secular Culture* (Boston: Beacon Press, 1987).

———. *The Word Made Flesh: A History of Christian Thought* (Oxford: Blackwell, 2004).

Miller, Robert J. (ed.), *The Complete Gospels* (San Francisco: HarperSanFrancisco, 1992).

Pagels, Elaine, *Beyond Belief: The Gospel of Thomas* (New York: Vintage Books, 2004).

———. *The Gnostic Gospels* (New York: Random House, 2004 reprint).

Patterson, Stephen J., *Beyond the Passion: Rethinking the Death and Life of Jesus* (Minneapolis: Augsburg Fortress, 2004).

———. *The God of Jesus: The Historical Jesus and the Search for Meaning* (Harrisburg, PA: Trinity Press International, 1988).

Robinson, James (ed.), *The Nag Hammadi Library in English* (San Francisco: HarperSanFrancisco, 1990).

Rudolph, Kurt, *Gnosis: The Nature and History of Gnosticism* (San Francisco: HarperSanFrancisco, 1987).

Valantasis, Richard, *Centuries of Holiness* (New York: Continuum, 2005).

———. *The Gospel of Thomas* (London: Routledge, 1997).

———. *The New Q: Translation and Commentary* (Harrisburg, PA: Trinity Press International, 2005).

————. *Religions of Late Antiquity in Practice* (Princeton: Princeton University Press, 2000).

Williams, Michael Allen, *Rethinking "Gnosticism"* (Princeton: Princeton University Press, 1999).

© Gary Isaacs

RICHARD VALANTASIS is the Clifford E. Baldridge Professor of New Testament and Christian Origins at the Iliff School of Theology in Denver, Colorado. He is the author of several books, including *Spiritual Guides of the Third Century*, *The Gospel of Thomas*, and *The New Q: A Fresh Translation and Commentary*. An ordained Episcopal priest, Valantasis is well known for his translations and analyses of the New Testament and esoteric writings. He lives in Denver, Colorado.

Beliefnet is the leading multifaith spirituality and religion website. Through its newsletters and online, Beliefnet reaches four million people daily. It is the winner of numerous prestigious awards, including the Webby for Best Spirituality Site and the Online News Association's top award for general excellence for independent websites. Its book *Taking Back Islam* won the Wilbur Award for Best Religion Book of 2003.